Marketing

Professional Reading Skills Series

*Accounting   M Sneyd
*Advertising   M-J St John
International Banking and Finance   M Sneyd
Marketing   M-J St John

* not yet published

English for Academic Purposes Series

Agriculture   C St J Yates
Business Studies   C Vaughan James
Computer Science   T Walker
Earth Sciences   C St J Yates
Economics   C St J Yates
General Engineering   D & C M Johnson
Medicine   D V James

Other titles of interest

Business Management English: Finance   J Comfort & N Brieger
**Business Management English: Language Reference for
   Business English**   N Brieger & J Comfort
Business Management English: Marketing   J Comfort & N Brieger
Business Management English: Personnel   N Brieger & J Comfort
Business Management English: Production and Operations   N Brieger & J Comfort

Professional Reading Skills Series

MARKETING

Maggie-Jo St John

Prentice Hall

New York   London   Toronto   Sydney   Tokyo   Singapore

PRENTICE HALL INTERNATIONAL ENGLISH LANGUAGE TEACHING

First published 1992 by
Prentice Hall International (UK) Ltd
Campus 400, Maylands Avenue
Hemel Hempstead
Hertfordshire, HP2 7EZ
A division of
Simon & Schuster International Group

Typeset in 10/12 pt Triumvirate
by MHL Typesetting Ltd, Coventry

Printed in Great Britain by Redwood Books,
Trowbridge, Wiltshire

Library of Congress Cataloging-in-Publication Data

St John, Maggie-Jo.
  Marketing / Maggie-Jo St John.
    p. cm. — (Professional reading skills series)
  Includes bibliographical references and index.
  ISBN 0-13-720046-3
  1. Readers—Marketing.   2. English language—Business English.
3. Marketing—Problems, exercises, etc.   4. English language-
-Textbooks for foreign speakers.   I. Title.   II. Series.
PE1127.B86S7   1992   91-39619
428.6'4'024658—dc20   CIP

British Library Cataloguing in Publication Data

A catalogue record for this book is available from the British Library

  ISBN 0-13-720046-3

---

2 3 4 5   95 94 93

Contents

Acknowledgements

All the material in this book appears with the permission of those who hold the copyright. The author and publishers thank the following for their permission to reproduce extracts of the copyright material.

Cobuild for definitions from *Collins Cobuild English Language Dictionary*; The Financial Times for *Old cars get a new lease of life*, John Griffiths 3 April 1991, *Premier seeks a premium with an innovative brew*, Harris Clay 24 January 1991, *Marketing is good for you*, Dalby Stewart 14 December 1990 and *Reincarnation in the Design Studio*, Andrew Fisher 3 April 1990; Haymarket Marketing Publications Ltd for *How shelf space made ecover*, Howard Gray in *Marketing* 18 October 1990, *Ralston-Purina entices breakfasts to run with the pack*, Laurel Tonby in *Marketing* 19 October 1990, *Heinzight*, Tom Lester in *Marketing* November 1990 and *No Smoke without Brand Fire*, Alan Mitchell 28 February 1991; Houghton Mifflin, Boston, US for *Exchange Relationships Marketing* and *Marketing*, Pride and Farrell 1987; Marketing Week for *V and A refreshes the arts*, 30 November 1990; Pan Books, London for *Marketing Mix, Is Price all that Matters, Give Benefits Not Products, Matching Products and Markets, Placing goods in the market place, What Routes could lead to our Customers?*, in *Introducing Marketing*, Wills G et al 1984; Prentice Hall, Englewood Cliffs NJ for *Marketing in/for Developing Countries*, Kinsey, *The Promotion Mix, Person Marketing, Breaking into an unreceptive market*, and *The World's Champion Marketers: the Japanese?*, in *Marketing* (second edition), Kotler and Armstrong, *Marketing*, Kotler, *How price signals quality, Marketing Today*, Kotler and Armstrong, *Branding Marketing Today*, (third edition), Oliver Gordon; V & A for Ace Caff posters.

Introduction

General information

English is often used in specialist journals, books and magazines to reach an international public. This book is one of a series which is designed to develop your reading skills and improve your familiarity with how English is used in particular professional areas of work.

The book contains texts, exercises and an answer key. It is accompanied by a cassette so that you can also listen to the reading texts being read aloud.

Using the book

The units
Each unit of the book contains one or more texts and a range of activities. These become more difficult so you will probably benefit most from working through the units in order. However, it is possible to use the units in any order. To help you see links and relationships, reference is sometimes made to a similar activity in a previous unit; you do not need to have done that activity but it may help you if you have.

Reading techniques
Before reading a text we suggest that you think about the topic; there are often pre-reading questions to help you do this. Then practise the techniques of skimming and scanning: skimming involves quickly finding the main ideas, usually by looking at the first and last paragraphs and the first sentences of other paragraphs; scanning is looking through the text for particular information, usually looking for key words, dates, numbers, etc., that is, information which can be found by running your eye up and down the page rather than along each line. Skim and scan questions are given before the text. All this prepares you for understanding the details of the text, extracting information from it and answering specific questions.

Using the cassette

Why listen?
The texts are read aloud by a native speaker of English so that you can relate the sound of the spoken word to the written word. English is not always pronounced as it is spelt and so it can be difficult to recognise, in conversation, words you have learnt through reading and vice versa. Also, there is evidence that suggests that our brains store words according to how they sound, so if you know how they sound you may remember and

recall them more easily. Hearing a text while following the written version can also improve comprehension.

What to listen for

Listen for groups of words and think why they are grouped together. Notice the pauses and changes of tone in the voice; these can help you identify different ideas and parts of the text and to recognise the transition from one part to the next. The stress given to words can also be an indication of their importance.

When to listen

It is often useful to listen to the cassette recording of the text after skimming and scanning and before a closer reading. At this stage, listen to the recording just once while you follow the text in the book. Then do the activities. After completing the exercises, you may like to listen to the recording several times, both with the text in front of you and without it.

The texts

Sources

The texts are taken from a range of recent publications such as books, magazines and newspapers. They have not been written for language learning but for people in professional fields to communicate with each other. They have been selected to cover a range of topics but also to show different kinds of writing. In some texts, the language is quite formal; in others it is more like speech and contains a lot of casual (colloquial) expressions, and you may only need to understand the general meaning of these.

Some of the texts were written and published in the United States and use American spelling. This should not affect you when reading, but when you write you should be consistent and either always use American spelling or always use British spelling.

Text types

The information, the order in which it occurs and the type of language depend on who the texts were written for (the audience) and why the text was written (the purpose). Texts will vary according to whether they are written for students, specialists or the general public and whether the intention is to explain, advertise, persuade, etc. As well as the information and the order in which it is presented, the choice of language and words will depend on the audience and the purpose. Thinking about these issues when you first meet a text can help you to understand it better.

The exercises

These are divided into five main categories: the first two are presented before the text. The questions that come after the text require you to read more carefully and will help you understand the information and learn more about the language. It is important to be able to explain how you reached an answer and what part(s) of the text you used as this shows deep, rather than surface, understanding.

In the main, there are three kinds of activities after the text. Not every text has questions of each kind or the same number of questions. The exercises reflect the type of text and the language and meaning in it. So, for instance, one text may have lots of Vocabulary questions but no Text Organisation ones. However, in each unit you will find there is a range of activities. The usual order is Text organisation, Comprehension, Vocabulary. This is because you should learn to see the text as a whole message rather than as a series of words.

Pre-reading
The first text in each unit is always preceded by pre-reading questions. These are designed to set you thinking about the particular topic because this will help you understand the text. Some but not all of the other texts have pre-reading questions, too. If you have already read one or more texts you will already be thinking and focusing on the topic and so extra questions may not be necessary.

Skimming and scanning
As already mentioned, when we have a text to read it is often helpful and time-saving to skim read it first; that is, glance at it very quickly just to get an overall idea of what the text is about. At other times, we only want to extract some specific information from the text and so we just scan; that is, look very quickly for words associated with our information. These are techniques which are useful when reading in any language and which improve with practice. Before each text you will find two or three skim and scan questions and you should aim to find the answers in just a few seconds.

Text organisation
These questions are to help you see how the writer has organised the information. There are certain patterns and conventions which develop the structure of the text and it is easier to understand the detailed information if you can follow the general way in which it is organised. This is a good point at which to think about the audience and purpose. This can also help you to see ways to organise your own writing.

Comprehension questions
These are to help you understand the important information and, often, to record it in note form using tables, lists, etc. Some questions can be answered by looking at just one part of the text; to answer others you will have to select and relate information from different parts of the text. You may be asked to write short answers, to underline information in the text, to decide if statements are true or false, to match, to order, to complete lists, charts, tables or to fill in gaps, etc. Where the exercise requires you to fill in a table or gaps, a standard size space has been left; the size of the space and length of the gap does not indicate the number or length of the missing word(s).

Vocabulary questions
These are aimed to help you understand the texts more fully as well as to help you to acquire a wider vocabulary. Specialised words are marked with an asterisk(*) and their meaning can be found in the Glossary at the back of the book. In addition, it is important that students become sensitive to whether words are formal or informal so that they use them in the correct context, and this aspect is practised. The concept of metaphor is also introduced and worked with. Metaphor is so much a feature of journalistic writing and is therefore vital to anyone who wishes to read newspapers and magazines. Some questions deal with the meaning of individual words but most deal with words in relation to each other. Learning isolated words can make it difficult to know how to use them. If you learn words as phrases and sets of related items then

you will find it easier to remember and use them. One sort of vocabulary activity involves Word Partnerships: many words are used in fairly specific combinations or partnerships. You will find it easier and more useful to remember partnerships rather than individual words.

In some units there are other types of questions such as **Text comparison** and **Viewpoints**. Text comparison focuses your attention on the features of different texts. Viewpoint may ask you about the author's or your view of a topic.

Answer key

As the activities have been carefully designed to help you learn as much as possible about the language and the topic, the answers are important. You should think about them carefully and think about *how* you reached your answer. The actual answer applies only to that text. The process by which you reached your answer can be applied to many texts and so there is more to be learnt from that.

The answer key does not usually contain answers to the pre-reading questions as they are to do with your knowledge and opinion rather than particular facts. Where there is only one factual answer this is given.

Where you are asked to write words or expressions and fill in gaps there is often more than one suitable answer. Those in the answer key should be seen as representative only; others of similar meaning would be equally acceptable. It is understanding the texts and learning from them that is important, not using exactly the same words as are suggested in the answer key.

Using these books in class

Students in a class can benefit from working on the exercises with a partner or in a small group of three or four. The discussion that results helps students to learn, especially if they have to explain their answer and how they reached it. When a question is causing difficulties students working in a small group can help each other and work towards a suitable answer. This helps them to become less dependent on the teacher.

Unit 1 Marketing concepts

In this unit there are three short texts all related to the basic concepts of marketing. They are taken from different sources and are written in different styles.

Text 1.1 What is marketing?

Pre-reading:
List five key words which you might meet in this text.

Skim and scan:
(a) Which paragraph defines marketing?
(b) Name two physical needs.

What is Marketing?

1   What does the term marketing really mean? Many people mistakenly think of it as advertising and selling. Given the number of commercials on television, in magazines and newspapers and all the signs and offers in and around the shops this is not surprising. However, advertising and selling are only two of several marketing functions, and not necessarily the most important ones. 5

2   The most basic concept underlying marketing is that of human needs. We have many needs including ones such as affection, knowledge and a sense of belonging as well as the physical need for food, warmth and shelter. A good deal of our lives is devoted to obtaining what will satisfy those needs. Marketing can thus be defined as any human activity which is directed at 10 satisfying needs and wants by creating and exchanging goods and value with others.

3   Marketing has become a key factor in the success of western businesses. Today's companies face stiff competition and the companies which can best satisfy customer needs are those which will survive and make the largest 15 profits.

Text organisation

1. Choose a heading for each paragraph:
    What to market   What marketing is not
    What marketing is   Where to market
    Reasons for marketing

Comprehension

2. Decide which of the following statements are True or False and give a paragraph number to show where your information came from.

   (a) Advertising is a part of marketing.
   (b) Selling is the most important function of marketing.
   (c) A sense of belonging is a physical need.
   (d) Satisfying customer needs is a key to success.

3. Complete this second definition of marketing by writing **one word** in each gap.

   Marketing is a process by which _____ obtain what they _____ and want by _____ goods or services.

Text 1.2 develops a key theme in the above definition of marketing, namely that of the process of exchange.

Text 1.2   Exchange relationships

Skim and scan:
   (a) How many conditions does the writer mention?
   (b) What do 'somethings of value' usually include?
   (c) What is the 'marketing mix'?

Exchange Relationships

1   Marketing consists of individual and organizational activities that facilitate and expedite satisfying exchange relationships in a dynamic environment through the creation, distribution, promotion and pricing of goods, services, and ideas. The four variables, creation, distribution, promotion, and pricing are called the *marketing mix*.   5

Fig. 1.1

2 | For an **exchange** to take place, four conditions must exist. First, an exchange requires participation by two or more individuals, groups, or organizations. Second, each party must possess something of value that the other party desires. Third, each must be willing to give up its 'something of value' to receive the 'something of value' held by the other. The objective 10 of a marketing exchange is to receive something that is desired more than what is given up to get it, that is, a reward in excess of costs. Fourth, the parties to the exchange must be able to communicate with each other to make their 'somethings of value' available.* The process of exchange is illustrated in Figure 1.1. As the arrows indicate, the two parties communicate to make 15 their 'somethings of value' available to each other. Note, though, that an exchange will not necessarily take place just because these four conditions exist. However, even if there is no exchange, marketing activities still have occurred. The 'somethings of value' held by the two parties are most often products and/or financial resources such as money or credit. When an 20 exchange occurs, products are traded for either other products or financial resources.

* Philip Kotler, *Marketing Management: Analysis, Planning, and Control*, 6th ed. (Englewood Cliffs, NJ: Prentice-Hall, 1984), p.8.

'Exchange Relationships Marketing' Pride and Farrell, (Houghton Mifflin) 1987

Comprehension

1. This text also includes a definition of marketing. Look at this definition and the two in Text 1.1 and its questions.

   (a) Find the other words used for *human* activity.   Definition 2 _____
                                                      Definition 3 _____
   (b) Find the other phrases used for goods and value.   Definition 2 _____
                                                      Definition 3 _____
   (c) What three other activities does definition 3 add to the *creation* of goods?

2. Summarise the four conditions the writer considers necessary for exchange. For each condition use a maximum of five words.
3. In Figure 1.1 six labels have been omitted. Where would you put the following labels?

Buyer   Something of value   Goods/services
Something of value   Money/labour/credit   Seller

4. In lines 1–2, what is the difference between 'facilitate' and 'expedite'?
5. (a) The marketing mix is often referred to as 'The 4 Ps'. In that expression can you think which words are used for (i) creation
                                                (ii) distribution?
    (If you have difficulty consult Text 1.3.)
   (b) Label each of the boxes in Figure 1.2 on page 4.

Fig. 1.2

The final text in this unit illustrates how the marketing mix was applied by the manufacturers of whisky.

Text 1.3 Marketing is good for you: revival in the fortunes of Scotch whisky

Pre-reading:
What brands of whisky do you know of?
What are some of the major companies producing whisky?
What kind of retailers would you buy whisky from?

Skim and scan:
The main topic of this text is

(a) whisky
(b) marketing
(c) Guinness
(d) selling

Text organisation

1. The underlying structure of this text is that of a PROBLEM and its SOLUTION.

(a) The problem arose (when?) _____
(b) The cause(s) of the problem was/were _____
(c) The problem was _____
(d) Guinness began to make changes (when?) _____
(e) The main steps taken were (i) _____
                            (ii) _____
                           (iii) _____
(f) The main solution was to _____

4

Marketing is good for you: revival in the fortunes of Scotch whisky

It is difficult to imagine a product more closely associated with a particular country than Scotch whisky.

One never hears of people going into a public house or restaurant and asking for an Irish. Yet Scotch whisky is universally known by its generic term of Scotch.

Whisky, from the Gaelic *uisge beatha* or literally, water of life, has been made in Scotland since the fifth century.

By the mid-1980s, however, the industry was static, with vast stocks hanging over the market and the value of sales going nowhere.

The consensus of opinion was that this was because of a concentration on production and volume with not enough attention being paid to selling. It is ironic that with such a well-known brand name, it was a failure of marketing which pushed the industry into the doldrums.

The situation began to change with the mergers and takeovers of the mid-1980s.

There were a number of moves to form Allied Distillers which is now part of Allied-Lyons. But it was the Guinness takeover of Bells and then Distillers to form United Distillers which really got the industry moving.

The mothballing of many distilleries helped reduce the lake, and United Distillers limited its sales of whisky to other distilleries, writing off large stocks on its balance sheet. It then concentrated on aggressively marketing bottled blended brands such as Johnnie Walker. With the surpluses reduced, prices were able to rise.

The 1989 Guinness annual report has a chapter entitled 'Brand marketing: the key to success'.

It says: 'After two years of radical reorganisation to streamline and restructure worldwide distribution operations, we have gained more effective control of the marketing of our key brands in major world markets.

'The focus of marketing effort on premium and de luxe brands together with our strong pricing policy reflect an overall policy of margin improvement within our business . . .'

Guinness clearly sees an important part of its revival as the marketing of well-known brands of Scotch.

But Dr Chris Greig, managing director of Invergordon Distillers, is pursuing a different line. Invergordon has four malt whiskies and Mackinlay, but the latter is not a household name as Scotch whiskies go. But the lion's share of its business comes from supplying blended whisky for own brands in supermarkets and other stores.

Dr Greig reckons that his company has done well as drinking habits have changed — people now buy whisky in supermarkets under own brand names, whereas once whisky was mostly bought in public houses.

Not only blended whiskies have flourished in the 1980s. Malt whiskies have become a successful niche product.

They are sold on cachet, status, and pedigree almost like fine wines, albeit on a smaller scale. Malts account for just over 7 per cent of the world Scotch market by value but only 4 per cent by volume.

'Financial Times' 14 December 1990

Comprehension

2. Look back to the 4 Ps mentioned on page 3:

    (a) Which variables of the marketing mix were particularly used by United Distillers?
    (b) Which variable did Invergordon Distillers use?
    (c) Which variable have neither of them mentioned explicitly?

Vocabulary

3. Which of the following are brand names?

    Whisky, Scotch, Johnnie Walker, Malt, Mars, Coca Cola, Orange Juice

4. Newspaper articles often use colloquial, colourful and pictorial language. Use the dictionary definitions and the text to try to work out the meaning of these expressions in the text:

    line 15   hanging over
    line 16   going nowhere
    line 24   doldrums
    line 34   mothballing
    line 35   lake
    line 37   writing off

---

hang over   1 If something such as a problem **hangs over** you, it worries you a lot. EG *I had the Open University examination hanging over me . . . the threat of deportation hanging over me.* V+PREP
2 A **hangover** is an idea, attitude, or state of mind which existed in the past but which is no longer important or relevant now. EG *You've still got this hangover of ideas . . . That sort of thinking is a hangover from the past.* N COUNT
3 Someone who is **hungover** feels tired and ill because they have drunk too much alcohol; an informal word. EG *I felt really hungover this morning, although I only had two pints last night.* ADJECTIVE
4 If you have a **hangover**, you feel tired and ill because you have drunk too much alcohol. N COUNT

nowhere /nəuwɛə/. **1** You use **nowhere** to make negative statements about places, for example to say that a suitable or appropriate place does not exist. EG *There was nowhere to hide . . . She had absolutely nowhere else to go . . . 'Where are we going?' — 'Nowhere in particular.' . . . Nowhere have I seen any serious mention of this.* ADV WITH VB: NEG = no place
2 If you say that something or someone appears **from nowhere** or **out of nowhere**, you mean that they have appeared suddenly and that you do not know where they have come from. EG *Two men suddenly appeared from nowhere . . . There were sudden rivers formed out of nowhere.* PHR:USED AS AN A = out of the blue
3 If you say that a place is **in the middle of nowhere**, you mean that it is isolated and a long way from anywhere civilized or interesting; an informal expression. EG *We were sitting in* PHR:USED AS AN A = in the sticks

---

the middle of nowhere ... a little village in the middle of nowhere.

4 If you say that you **are nowhere**, that you **are getting nowhere**, or that something **is getting** you **nowhere**, you mean that all your efforts are unsuccessful and are not producing any worthwhile results. EG *I keep going off on tangents that get me nowhere ... Calling me yellow will get you nowhere ... without them I would be nowhere.*

PHR:VB
INFLECTS

5 If you say that something is **nowhere near** the case, you mean that it is not true at all, and that the truth is quite different. EG *Lions are nowhere near as fast as the cheetah.*

PHR:NEG PHR+
as...as

doldrums /dɒldrəmz/. If an activity or situation is **in the doldrums**, it is very quiet and nothing new or exciting is happening. EG *The American market is as much in the doldrums as the British one ... By and large, athletics were in the doldrums during the 1960s.*

PHR:USED AS AN
A
⇑ inactive
= in a rut

mothball /mɒθbɔːl/, **mothballs**. A **mothball** is a small white ball made of a chemical such as naphthalene, which you can put amongst clothes or blankets in order to keep moths away and prevent them from making holes in them.

N COUNT

lake /leɪk/, **lakes**. A **lake** is a large area of fresh water, surrounded by land. EG *On the edge of the lake was a pavilion.* ▶ Used as part of a name. EG *... the calm waters of Lake Michigan ... ... the Great Lakes separating Canada and America.*

N COUNT
▶ N IN NAMES

write off **1** If you **write off** to a company or organization, you send them a letter, usually asking them to send you one of their products or information about their products. EG *I've written off for a set of special pens I saw advertised in the paper. He sat down and wrote off letters in answer to the advertisements.*

PHRASAL VB:V+
ADV OR V+O+
ADV

2 If someone **writes off** a debt or an amount of money that has been spent on a project, they accept that they are never going to get the money back. EG *Unless the debts can be re-scheduled or written off, the world will soon face a financial crisis ... He urged the government to write off the corporation's losses.*

PHRASAL VB:V+
O+ADV
⇑ forget

3 If you **write off** a plan or project, you accept that it is not going to be successful and do not continue with it.

PHRASAL VB:V+
O+ADV
= ditch

4 If you **write** someone **off**, you decide that they are unimportant or useless and that they are not worth further serious attention. EG *Do not sound harassed, or you will be written off as a hysterical woman.*

PHRASAL VB:V+
O+ADV.
⇑ reject
= dismiss

5 If someone **writes off** a vehicle, they have a crash in it and it is so badly damaged that it is not worth repairing.

PHRASAL VB:V+
O+ADV

6 See also **write-off**.

Text comparison

1. Where do you think each of the extracts is from?

    Newspaper   Journal   Student textbook   Magazine   Encyclopaedia
    Book   Dictionary

2. Draw up a table showing features of each text. You might like to consider some of the following aspects:

    Length of paragraphs   Vocabulary — formal/informal
    Length of sentences   Vocabulary — neutral/colourful
    Use of definitions   Readability, for you
    Use of references   Interest, for you

	Text 1.1	Text 1.2	Text 1.3
Source			
Typical features			

Unit 2 Products

In this unit there are three texts. Two come from the same source. Can you work out which two come from the same source?

Text 2.1 Give benefits not products

Pre-reading:
What purpose do the following things fulfil for you? i.e. Why do you buy them?

toothpaste
light bulbs
batteries

Skim and scan:
(a) What is the main point the writer makes in the first two paragraphs?
(b) Why is product orientation considered too narrow?
(c) What is 'marketing myopia'?

Give benefits not products

1 Successful marketers try to remain open and flexible, yet there is one unchanging maxim which they share: *customers don't buy products; they seek to acquire benefits*. Those few words hold the secret of many an innovative organisation's success. It is a principle which can be applied to almost any product/market decision. 5

2 The principle itself is almost deceptively simple, which is why some marketers pass it by. The successful marketing organisation will pay more than lip service to its meaning, because it represents the most basic yet most important principle of marketing. Customers do not buy a product for the product itself. Customers buy clean floors, not floor polish. They buy security, 10 not insurance policies; high performance engines (or status), not Ferraris; better lubrication, not industrial cutting oil.

3 An innovative tool manufacturer realised, through the course of its relationship with its customers, that a major problem on the production floor was the time lost in changing abrasive discs. The company invested a great 15 deal of time and money in seeking a solution, and invented a highly specialised system of binding grit to disc. The result was a new disc which had a much longer life and could be removed and replaced much faster than the old type.

9

This gave the organisation's customers the benefit of more efficient production time and better value for money. [20]

4   The benefit in the last example served a dual purpose; it gave the customer the advantage of time-saving and cost-effectiveness, and at the same time solved a traditional problem of changing discs. The 'problem' in this case was a customer need which had to be satisfied.

5   The concept of customer benefits shows the importance of an organisation [25] being orientated towards the customer, or market, rather than the product. The organisation cannot afford to adopt a narrow view of its role by concentrating only on the product. An organisation, for example, manufacturing adding machines in a marketing environment which is moving towards calculators will soon find itself and its product obsolete. It must [30] consider what the benefits of its product are — in this case computing sums accurately and quickly — and make sure that it is providing that benefit better than any other organisation. If a better or more cost-effective method of computing comes along, the customer will naturally be attracted to that product which incorporates those developments and can therefore provide [35] increased benefits.

6   Marketers must be on guard against what one marketing specialist has termed 'marketing myopia'. Theodore Levitt described this condition as the result of confusing products with markets.

7   The organisation can avoid myopia of this kind by maintaining a dynamic [40] and regular check on its product range. It must constantly assess its product by asking: 'Does the product provide the relevant and desired benefits to meet our customers' needs today?'

'Introducing Marketing' Wills, G., et al (Pan Books) 1984

Comprehension

1. (a) Copy Table A into your notebook, allowing space for further examples. Record the products named in the second paragraph and the corresponding benefit.

Table A

	Products	Benefits
Paragraph 2	(a) (b) (c) (d)	

(b) Can you find more examples in the passage to add to Table A? Can you add any examples of your own?

2. What do the following refer to?

   (a) line 3 'those few words'
   (b) line 17 'the result'
   (c) line 19 'this'

Vocabulary

3. What is the meaning of:

   line 2 maxim   (a) words
                        (b) principle
                        (c) product
                        (d) benefit
   line 7 pass it by   (a) are unaware of it
                        (b) go past it
                        (c) do not choose it
                        (d) do not tell others
   line 8 lip service (a) disapprove
                        (b) approve
                        (c) pretend to approve
                        (d) pretend to disapprove

4. The words or phrases below could replace words or phrases used in the text. Write out the exact word(s) in the text that could be replaced and give the line number. (The words occur in the same order as the list.)

e.g. just mentioned	in the last example	line 21
simultaneously		
longstanding		
out of date		
includes		
careful to avoid		
mixing up		
an ongoing		

Text 2.2 Matching products and markets

Matching products and markets

1   Marketing has been defined as the process of matching an organisation's
resources with customer needs. The result of this process is a product. The
need, therefore, for the organisation to remain dynamic is obvious because
the product is the only key to the organisation's solvency and profitability.
No matter how else the organisation runs itself cost-effectively and sensibly,   5
if the product is not selling well then the money simply will not be coming
in. Company and consumer are interdependent.

2   Successful product management depends on the organisation knowing how
and if the current product range meets consumer and organisational
objectives. One way of doing this, as previously described, is to conduct   10
detailed benefit analysis segmentation.

3   The most important attitude towards product management is to view the
product as only one part of the marketing mix which also includes price,
place and promotion. In this way, the product is viewed as a variable which
can be adapted or even changed radically to meet a changing market. How   15
it can be changed will depend on several factors within and outside the
organisation, including the organisation's resources, market conditions and
opportunities and competitive threats.

Product-market strategy

4   'Product-market strategy' is the term used to describe all the decisions which   20
the organisation makes about its target markets and the products it offers
to those markets. The use of the word 'strategy' is important, for it implies
a chosen route to a defined goal and suggests long-term planning. This is
quite different from 'tactical' activities which are used to achieve short-term
objectives by gaining immediate results. Product-market strategy represents   25
a decision about the current and future direction of the organisation.

5   Product-market strategy must be developed in the most cost-effective
manner, paying attention to cash flow and profitability requirements. To
minimise costs at the outset, a sound marketing approach will usually attempt
to increase profits and cash flow from existing markets. The following   30
examples can help illustrate the total strategy at work.

6   *Market penetration*   Heinz revamped its marketing strategy to increase
consumption of its tinned soups. This product was traditionally a winter
purchase, but Heinz successfully promoted the idea of celery soup, drunk
hot or cold, as a suitable summer purchase. The product attributes of celery   35
were linked with concepts of slimming and refreshment on summer days.

7   *Market development*   A British hotel chain opened up a new market by
offering 'Leisure Learning' weekends in its hotels.

8   *Product range extension*   A European breakfast cereal manufacturer brought out a new 'variety' pack to appeal to young children who liked the 40 freedom of choosing a new cereal each morning.

9   *Product development*   Manufacturers of digital watches soon combined the watch function with an alarm component. This not only attracted customers who liked the novelty of the idea, but seriously threatened the traditional watch market.   45

'Introducing Marketing' Wills, G., et al (Pan Books) 1984

Text organisation

1. Compare the definition of marketing given here with the definitions in Unit 1.

    (a) What is similar?
    (b) What is different?

2. There is another definition.

    (a) Which part of the text does it come in?
    (b) What is being defined?

3. (a) What is similar about the position in the two texts of the two definitions?
    (b) Why do you think they come in these positions?

Comprehension

4. Why must an organisation be dynamic?
5. List the factors that affect product change as internal or external.

Internal	External

6. Explain the difference between strategy and tactics.
7. There are examples of four product–market strategies in the text. Which of those strategies do the following extra examples illustrate?

    (a) The production of new ice-cream bars based on traditional chocolate bars (such as Mars Bars, Snickers, Kit Kat).
    (b) Adding an automatic timer to a microwave oven.
    (c) Using cinemas and theatres for daytime talks.

Vocabulary

8. Word Partnerships: Many words are used in fairly specific combinations or partnerships. You will find it easier and more useful to remember partnerships rather than individual words, Pages 92—97 have been reserved for this at the back of the book. In some units you will be asked to search the texts and list the partnerships; in other units you are left to do this for yourself.

'Market' and the words derived from it occur in lots of partnerships, some of two words and others of three or more. Some of the partnerships in Texts 2.1 and 2.2 are:

Two-word partnerships	**Three-word partnerships**
target markets	product-market strategy
marketing environment	

Add to these lists and then see what you can find for 'product'

Text 2.3 Branding

Pre-reading:
What are the first five brand names you think of?
Compare these with the list written by your partner. Are any the same?

Skim and scan:
(a) Is the use of branding increasing or decreasing?
(b) Which was the top British brand in 1988?

Branding

1 Products can be sold as unbranded commodities. Raw materials are still treated in this way, but increasingly branding is becoming dominant, even in the supply of industrial components and in hitherto unbranded areas such as vegetables.

2 What is the power of brands? Would you buy unpackaged, unbranded breakfast cereal from an itinerant street-trader? Would you buy perfume as a present for a female relative if it came in an unlabelled brown bottle? Would you buy an anonymous microcomputer from an anonymous source? Branding saves us much time as consumers. A simple word or two comes to represent a wealth of associations, for us and for others, and can offer detailed expectations. So that we do not need to ponder on the possibly murky channels used by the trader in obtaining supplies of breakfast cereal. We know the female relative will like the perfume — she may have even previously specified the brand. We know the range of compatible software for the microcomputer. Consumers learn to place some reliance upon brand names when evaluating competing products. In services, too, branding can serve

the consumer by offering consistent, identifiable services which might reduce confusion and save on search time.

3   Marks & Spencer is the top brand in Britain according to a survey in 1988. It scored highest on awareness and on how highly regarded it was by members [20] of the public. An interesting comparison is between Britain and Europe. Top brands across Europe are dominated by car manufacturers. In all cases it is the corporate identity that dominates.

4   There are several options in brand strategy. A company can sell under its own brand or under that of another company. In the latter case it is often [25] a retailer's own label. In using the company's brand a choice will be needed between using a 'family' brand name for all that firm's brands, as opposed to giving each product an individual brand name.

5   Some companies attempt to obtain the benefits of both strategies by family branding and at the same time having several 'sub-brands'. Ford puts its name [30] on all its cars, which also have individual brand names. The Lever subsidiary Birds Eye Walls is now creating sub-brands in frozen foods with Menu Masters and Captain Birds Eye. An alternative trend is seen in Reckitt and Colman's food and wine division, where strong brands in several product fields (Colmans mustard, Gales honey, Jiff lemon, Robinson's barley water, [35] Moussec, Veuve du Vernay, Bulls Blood) are being brought under the umbrella of the corporate brand of Colmans of Norwich.

Table 2.3.1   *Survey of brand names*

Top brands in Britain	Top brands in Europe
1. Marks & Spencer	1. Mercedes
2. Cadbury	2. Philips
3. Kellogg	3. Volkswagen
4. Heinz	4. Rolls-Royce
5. Rolls-Royce	5. Porsche
6. Boots	6. Coca-Cola
7. Nescafé	7. Ferrari
8. BBC	8. BMW
9. Rowntree	9. Michelin
10. Sainsbury	10. Volvo

Source: Landor Associates.

'Branding Marketing Today' Gordon, O., (Prentice Hall) 3rd Edition

Comprehension

1. What are the benefits to us as customers of brand names?
2. Decide which of the following statements are True or False and give paragraph numbers to show where your information came from.

(a) Raw materials are sold as branded goods.
(b) Branding applies to goods and services.
(c) Rolls-Royce is well known and popular in Britain and Europe.
(d) The British seem more interested in food than the Europeans.
(e) A labelled brown bottle is a branded product.

3. Label the strategies in the classification tree and give examples where indicated:

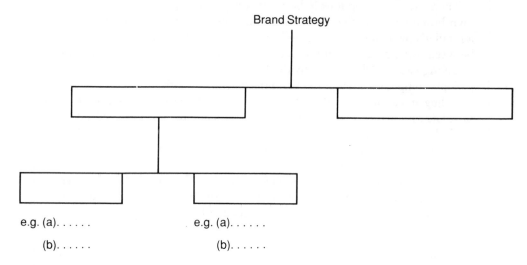

Brand Strategy

e.g. (a). . . . . .   e.g. (a). . . . . .
    (b). . . . .   (b). . . . . .

Vocabulary

4. Fill in the blanks with the correct expression.

   (a) Large retailers often get manufacturers to produce goods for them and then
       market these as _____ _____ goods.
   (b) 'Family brand name' and _____ _____ stand for the same thing.
   (c) Colman's have well known brands in a range of _____ _____.
   (d) Captain Birds Eye is a _____-_____ of the well known brand Birds
       Eye.

5. Which one(s) of the following would you associate with 'murky channels' (lines
   11–12)?

   (a) top quality goods
   (b) stolen goods
   (c) labelled goods
   (d) rejects

6. Select the best meaning in this text for each of the words below.

   line 6   itinerant   (a) regular
                            (b) travelling
                            (c) well established
                            (d) reputable

line 8   anonymous   (a) unreliable
                       (b) unusual
                       (c) unsound
                       (d) unnamed

line 14   compatible   (a) competing
                       (b) existing
                       (c) matching
                       (d) efficient

7. Word Relationships: Different endings on the same word-stem change the function
    of a word. Complete the table below. You can find some of the words you need
    in paragraphs 2 and 3 of the passage; others you may know or need to look up
    in a dictionary. (An 'x' in this type of activity means you need not try and find these
    less common words.)

Verb	Noun	Adjective
associate	representation	X
specify		X
identify		reliable
compare		
		dominant

Viewpoint

Author's intention:

8. In paragraph 2 the author asks some questions. Does he:

    (a) answer them directly
    (b) answer them indirectly
    (c) not answer them at all?

9. Why do you think the author asks these questions?

    (a) because he is interested in your answers
    (b) so that he can answer them later in the text
    (c) to involve you and gain your attention

Unit 3 Place

In this unit there are three texts related to the *placing* or *distribution* of goods. The first discusses some key issues and the others provide examples of how distribution was planned for two different products. You will be asked at the end of the unit to say where you think each text comes from and why (cf. Unit 1).

Text 3.1 Placing goods in the market place

Pre-reading:
How many ways can you think of for goods to pass from a producer to a customer? Can you suggest any advantages or disadvantages of each way?

Skim and scan:
(a) How many sections is the text divided into?
(b) Choose, from the list below, a heading for each section:

The channel of distribution	Outlets
The four Ps	Routes
The importance of place	Intermediaries
Channel choice	Purchasing
Why use intermediaries?	

Placing goods in the market place

1 Our previous discussions of the marketing mix emphasised the need to understand the impact of the mix elements on an organisation's marketing effectiveness. However, it is often the case that organisations concentrate on three elements — product, price and promotion — and leave the fourth element, *place*, almost to look after itself. In the quartet of the 'P's, place 5 is the shorthand description for the means by which the matching process between the needs of the market and the offering of the firm is finally achieved by getting the product to the right place at the right time.

2 The channel of distribution is the route that a product takes (remembering that the word 'product' in our usage includes services) in reaching its end 10 users. Outlets must be created which enable the product and the customer to be physically brought together, and which enable the customer to buy.

3 Television advertising for a light travelling iron succeeded in interesting one would-be customer, known to the authors, who went along to Currys,

Dixons, Dickens and Jones and other likely shops on the assumption that 15
the iron would be in stock. It was not. The shops chosen had other travelling
irons, but not the brand that had been advertised. Was the customer going
to the wrong shops? Or had the producer advertised before sorting out
physical supply to retailers? Or had the producer failed to 'sell' the product
to the retailers? Whatever the reason, the lack of availability of the product 20
in the right place at the right time meant that a sale was lost; in the end,
the consumer settled for a competitor's brand.

4   Marketers who wish to avoid such miscalculations need to take into strategic
     account two main aspects of the channel of distribution.
5   — The trading route, through which the product is made available for 25
     purchase. This concerns the sequence of negotiation, buying and selling that
     goes on. Goods nowadays are sometimes bought and sold by intermediaries
     who never actually see or handle the merchandise; their task is to ensure that
     the product finds buyers, and then to effect sales.
6   — The route through which the product is physically moved from factory 30
     gate to end-user, by pallet-load and forklift, by crane and container lorry.
     This is the concern of physical distribution management as well as of
     marketing management: an interesting interface to which we shall return.
     The function of this aspect of the channel is to make the product available
     for *use*. Services, such as banking facilities, are not moved by the same means, 35
     but they nonetheless do need to be made available in a physical sense. Banks
     need to have branches, 24-hour cash tills and so on, that are convenient for
     customers to use, and these are channel considerations.

7   A fundamental issue regarding channels of distribution, whether on the
     trading or the physical side, is whether the producer should take the product 40
     direct to the end-user himself, or whether intermediaries should be used. For
     a variety of reasons that we shall soon come to, intermediaries are in fact
     used more often than not, and channels of distribution often amount to chains
     of such intermediaries.

8   The use of any intermediaries at all is bound to result in some degree of loss 45
     of direct contact with the market place and loss of control over key areas
     such as customer service policy. So why, in fact, are intermediaries used?
9   One reason for their use is that intermediaries specialise in particular
     activities. Hence, economies of specialisation are achieved and the channel
     as a whole benefits from division of labour. The intermediary may also achieve 50
     economies of scale through high volume at high throughput levels that are
     normally unavailable to a single firm doing the same tasks on its own account.
10   The use of intermediaries also reduces 'contactual costs'. These are the costs
     of the contacts that need to be made between buyers and sellers to distribute
     a product.   55

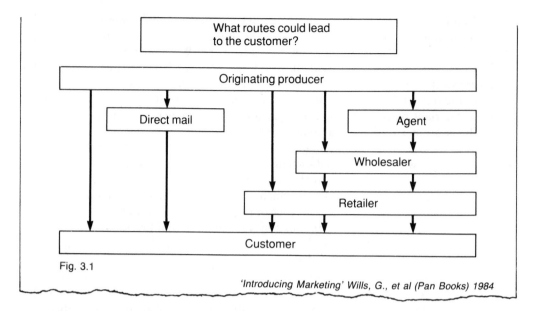

Fig. 3.1

'Introducing Marketing' Wills, G., et al (Pan Books) 1984

Comprehension

1. Give a short (e.g. about 15 words) definition of the marketing term, 'place'.

2. The author considers that 'place' is often neglected.

    (a) Give the sections and line numbers for **two** places where this view is expressed.
    (b) What example of poor placing is given?
    (c) What can be the results of poor placing?

3. (a) How many routes are there for the channel of distribution?
    (b) What are these called?
    (c) What is the purpose of each route?

4. Complete the table to show advantages and disadvantages of using intermediaries.

Advantages	Disadvantages

5. Read the examples below showing how two companies developed their channels of distribution. For each one draw a figure like Figure 3.1 in the text, showing the channel(s) the company was using, and is using now.

One international chemical company selling to Europe through its own sales office direct to customers found that the use of a chemical merchant or wholesaler would reduce selling costs and allow the company to take advantage of a ready-made sales organisation.

Another company, a British shoe manufacturer producing better-quality shoes, found that it could open up a new and profitable market segment by including its products in the catalogue of a national mail order firm. Soon the manufacturer was selling the same shoes, at the same prices, to two, largely distinct markets: to the up-market speciality shoe shop and to the wider down-market audience reached through the mail-order catalogue.

Vocabulary

6. Give one word which would have the opposite meaning to the following words as they are used in the text:

   Section 1   lines 3–4   concentrate on
   Section 2   line 21   lost
   Section 3   line 37   convenient

7. The following words have more than one meaning. Study the dictionary entries for each one and decide which meaning is used in this passage.

   Section 2   line 11   outlets
   Section 5   line 28   handle

outlet /aʊtlɪ²t/, **outlets**. An **outlet** is **1** a means of expressing and releasing emotions, feelings, or ideas which you have inside you. EG ... *outlets for political expression*. **2** a market for a product. EG *There is a huge sales outlet for pocket calculators.* **3** a shop or organization which sells the goods made by a particular manufacturer. EG *Several commercial outlets had already expressed an interest.* **4** a hole or pipe through which water or air can flow out. EG *Clean the sink outlet ... ... the outlet of the water supply.*	N COUNT = channel N COUNT N COUNT N COUNT ⇑ exit
handle /hændəˀl/, **handles, handling, handled. 1** A **handle** is **1.1** a lever or other small object that is attached to a door or window and is used for opening and closing it. EG *He tugged at the metal handle*. **1.2** the part of an object that you hold in order to carry it or use it. EG ... *a broom handle*.	N COUNT
2 If you **fly off the handle**, you suddenly and completely lose your temper.	PHRASE Informal
3 When you **handle** something, you hold it and move it about in your hands. EG *Glass. Handle with Care.*	V+O
4 When you **handle** something such as a weapon, car, or horse, you use or control it effectively. EG *She had handled a machine gun herself ... This car handles very nicely.*	V-ERG: IF V THEN+A
5 If you **handle** a problem or difficult situation, you deal with it successfully. EG *You don't have to come, Hendricks and I can handle it.* ◇ **handling**. EG *His handling of these important issues was condemned by the opposition.*	V+O ◇ N UNCOUNT: USU+*of*
6 If you **handle** a particular area of work, you have responsibility for it. EG *He handles all the major accounts.*	V+O
7 If you can **handle** people, you establish a good relationship with them so that they respect you and do what you want them to. EG *The principal was a genius in the way he handled us.*	V+O

8. Part of the meaning of the following words can be deduced from the first part (underlined) of the word.

   (a) What does the underlined part mean?
   (b) What does the word mean?

Section 1	line 5	<u>quart</u>et
3	line 13	<u>tele</u>vision
4	line 23	<u>mis</u>calculations
5	line 27	<u>inter</u>mediaries

Text 3.2 How shelf space made Ecover

Pre-reading:
What is a 'fad'?
What does the concept 'Green' mean today?
Do you know what else it means if you call someone green?

Skim and scan:
(a) What is Ecover?
(b) Which companies and what products does it compete with?
(c) Why has it been successful?
(d) Is the market for goods like Ecover contracting, static or growing?

How Shelf Space made Ecover

1

Ecover went from fad to major brand by being Green. Howard Gray shows how distribution played a key role in its success.

2   The Ecover story is most well known as that of being 'right product at the right time'. After all, in the space of two years it emerged from faddist obscurity to become a household name, with sales worth £9.5m. And along the way it has inspired a host of similar environmentally-friendly products.

3   But in one sense, the Ecover story is just as much one of selling to the dreaded supermarket buyers — the tale of how a small, previously unrecognised brand hit the big time by grabbing a presence on the multiples' shelves.

4   The company behind this particular side of the Ecover story is Ascot Management Group, a brokerage firm set up two years ago, which took responsibility for distributing the 'environmentally-friendly' washing powder. The company, which specialises in Green and organic products, is the brainchild of Simon Dunn, formerly sales director of Jordan's cereals business, and Stephen Jones, an ex-supermarket buyer.

5   Getting the products into the supermarket was crucial. Ecover's 2% share of the £600m washing powders and liquid cleaners market was achieved without recourse to TV and press advertising.

6   And while 2% may sound like pretty small beer, Ecover is up against some of the most sophisticated — and open fisted — marketers around. Procter and Gamble (Fairy Liquid and Ariel) and Lever Brothers (Persil) have been at loggerheads for decades — and no third party has previously managed to get so much as a look in.

7   'Luckily, the time was right in terms of the public readiness for the product. So when it appeared on the shelves, consumer interest — and sales — went from strength to strength', adds Dunn.

8   'Traditionally, margins on big-name washing powders have always been low; so here was an opportunity for the multiples to look both Green and make more money. How could they resist?'

9   Ascot is currently giving the same treatment to other Green and organic clients whose brands are known to health food *aficionados*

could just as easily dissolve, along with consumer interest in all things Green, since 75% of the company's brands fall into the eco-Green market. Dunn and Jones, however, disagree. They are predicting that the organic/Green market is set to quadruple over the next four years. 80 85

14

Certainly, the signs are clear that this is not just a passing fancy. Product innovation is increasing all the time, especially in the organic sector — Euromonitor recently predicted that the value of this market could quadruple by 1993. And the Germans are setting the pace in the EEC by planning a drastic reduction of plastic and paper waste through improved recycling. 90

Jones points out: 'We've used our knowledge of the grocery trade in order to catapult brands such as Ecover into the big time. It's a business, of course, like any other — but there's an added benefit to what we do in that the more products that we manage to sell, the better it is for the environment.' 95 100

15

And indeed in the 'caring sharing' 90s — a concept much vaunted in the planning departments of ad agencies — the talk is of just how important corporate image is going to become. 105

16

'Marketing' October 1990

but previously had no proper distribution in the grocery multiples. 55

10

These include the Paper Chain range of eco-friendly toilet tissues and kitchen towels; Cawston Vale soft drinks; and Meridian Foods, which produces a range of 'speciality' oils and organic, processed foods. A new sales and marketing arm called Product Chain will focus on developing both Green and non-Green brands. 60

11

'Buyers drive a hard bargain in this business', says Jones. 'They can be arrogant and difficult to deal with, but they're able to recognise a potential winner when they see one. You just have to stress the right benefits. I've got the advantage of having been a buyer for most of the major supermarket chains, and so I know the nature of the beast that I have to deal with.' 65 70

12

Of course, it could be argued that Ascot was just lucky. It was established in a climate which was particularly receptive to any product which could possibly claim Green credentials. 75

13

Taking that one step further, its success

Comprehension

1. What are the two 'stories' of Ecover?
2. Does Ascot Management Group manufacture Ecover? Use the text to explain your answer.
3. (a) What important experience did Stephen Jones have?
   (b) Why was this valuable?

4. What is a potential danger for Ascot?
5. Why are Dunn and Jones confident that there is nothing to worry about?

6. What is the benefit their product offers?
7. Complete the summary below. Each blank represents one word. The first set of blanks has been done for you as an example.

The distribution process is all about getting _____ _____ _____ to _____ _____ _____ at _____ _____ _____. An example of a _____ story in a very _____ area is that of the Ecover brands. They succeeded in _____ _____ the supermarket markets _____ the strong _____ of brands such as _____ _____ _____ _____/_____. This was partly a result of _____ _____ _____ _____ but also because of Jones' _____ of the business and what supermarket _____ want, which is a _____. Ascot did not need to use any _____ to promote their products. It seems that the _____ market is going to _____ in the next few years.

8. What do these words refer to?: line 16   the multiples
                                       lines 64–5   this business
                                       lines 86–7   this (is not just a passing fancy)
                                       line 90   this market

Vocabulary

9. The words in column A can mean the same as one or more words in the given paragraphs. Write the equivalent word(s) from the passage in column B and give the line number. The first one has been done for you as an example.

	Column A	Column B	
paragraph 2.	tale	story	line 5
	developed		
	many		
paragraph 3.	seizing		
paragraph 4.	established		
	previously		
paragraph 5.	vital		
	using		

10. The writer uses many idiomatic expressions. Match the expression in column A with a meaning from column B (note that there are more meanings than idiomatic expressions).

Column A (Expressions)		Column B (Meanings)
to hit the big time	line 15	in strong disagreement
small beer	lines 33–4	unimportant
to be at loggerheads	line 38	unsophisticated
a passing fancy	line 87	be successful
to catapult	line 97	short-term attraction
		launch very rapidly
		very firm

24

Text 3.3 Fast food

Pre-reading:
What do you understand by, and what examples can you give of, 'fast food'?

Fast food
Ralston-Purina entices breakfasts to run with the pack

1 The Americans have discovered another fast food — take-away breakfast cereals. Ralston-Purina, the sixth largest cereal-maker in the US, last week announced plans to test what it calls 'Breakfast on the Run', the first all-in-one cereal product.

2 Breakfast on the Run contains a single-serving box of cereal, a carton of long-life milk, a packet of sugar, a spoon and napkin — all for two dollars.

3 Individual serving packs themselves will raise no eyebrows in the US. Kellogg came out with the packs sometime in the 50s, but most cereal marketers abandoned them by the late 70s.

4 Since then, manufacturers in this $6.5bn (£3.4bn) industry had virtually ignored the convenience market, concentrating instead on reformulating their products to attract different audience segments. Lately their main pitch has been to emphasize the health and nutritional aspects of their brands.

5 Ralston could be eyeing the fast-food arena, which Kellogg and General Mills have already identified as a priority. This summer, both companies joined up with McDonald's to offer their cereals through its outlets.

'Marketing' October 1990

Comprehension

1. What makes 'Breakfast on the Run' an *all-in-one* product?
2. (a) Which items in the pack are not edible?
   (b) What do you do with them?
3. What other name is given to the fast food market?
4. What marketing techniques have cereal producers used in the past?
   and now they are using _____.

Viewpoint

5. How 'Green' do you think this product is?

Vocabulary

6. (a) 'To run with the pack' is an expression used in hunting. In this text what constitutes 'the pack'?
   (b) To 'raise your eyebrows' means _____.
   (c) What does 'to eye something' mean?
   (d) A 'pitch' is used in several sports. What is it and can you name some sports which use one? What is its meaning here in this text?

Text comparison

Where do you think each text comes from?
What are some of the features of the texts that help you to decide this?
(For ideas look back to the similar question at the end of Unit 1, page 8).
Draw up a table as in Unit 1.

Unit 4 Promotion

The theme of this unit is promotion, the one of the 4 Ps we are all familiar with from advertising. There is another book in this series which takes a more detailed look at the language of advertising and promotion.

Text 4.1 The promotion mix

Pre-reading:
Advertising is only one category of promotional activities.
Do you know any others?
What promotions, including advertisements, can you remember clearly?
Which ones have influenced you?

Skim and scan:
(a) How many categories of promotional activities are there?
(b) What are they?
(c) What is a key difference between public relations and advertising?

This text is divided into four sections. Read the whole text and then answer the questions on each section.

The Promotion Mix

1   *Advertising* ▪ Because of the many forms and uses of advertising, it is hard to generalize about its unique qualities as a part of the promotion mix. Yet several qualities can be noted. Advertising's public nature suggests that the advertised product is standard and legitimate. Because many people see ads for the product, buyers know that purchasing the product will be publicly   5 understood and accepted. Advertising also lets the seller repeat a message many times, and it lets the buyer receive and compare the messages of various competitors. Large-scale advertising by a seller says something positive about the seller's size, popularity, and success.

2   Advertising is also very expressive, letting the company dramatize its   10 products through the artful use of print, sound, and color. On the one hand, advertising can be used to build up a long-term image for a product (such as Coca-Cola ads) and, on the other, to trigger quick sales (as when K mart advertises a weekend sale). Advertising can reach masses of geographically spread-out buyers at a low cost per exposure.   15

3   Advertising also has some shortcomings. Although it reaches many people quickly, advertising is impersonal and cannot be as persuasive as a company salesperson. Advertising is able to carry on only a one-way communication with the audience, and the audience does not feel that it has to pay attention or respond. In addition, advertising can be very costly. Although some forms, 20 such as newspaper and radio advertising, can be done on small budgets, other forms, such as network TV advertising, require very large budgets.

1   *Personal selling* ■ Personal selling is the most effective tool at certain stages of the buying process, particularly in building up buyers' preferences, convictions, and actions. As compared with advertising, personal selling has several unique qualities. It involves personal interaction between two or more people, so each person can observe the other's needs and characteristics and 5 make quick adjustments. Personal selling also lets all kinds of relationships spring up, ranging from a matter-of-fact selling relationship to a deep personal friendship. The effective salesperson keeps the customer's interests at heart in order to build a long-run relationship. Finally, the buyer usually feels a greater need to listen and respond, even if the response is a polite 'no thank 10 you'.

2   These unique qualities come at a cost. A salesforce requires a longer-term commitment than advertising — advertising can be turned on and off, but salesforce size is harder to change. And personal selling is the company's most expensive promotion tool, costing industrial companies an average of $197 15 per sales call. American firms spend up to three times as much on personal selling as they do on advertising.

1   *Sales promotion* ■ Sales promotion includes a wide assortment of tools — coupons, contests, cents-off deals, premiums, and others — and these tools have many unique qualities. They attract consumer attention and provide information that may lead the consumer to buy the product. They offer strong incentives to purchase by providing inducements or contributions that give 5 additional value to consumers. And sales promotions invite and reward quick response. While advertising says 'buy our product,' sales promotion says 'buy it now.'

2   Companies use sales-promotion tools to create a stronger and quicker response. Sales promotion can be used to dramatize product offers and to 10 boost sagging sales. However, sales-promotion effects are usually short-lived and are not effective in building long-run brand preference.

1   *Public Relations* ■ Public relations offers several unique qualities. It is very believable — news stories, features, and events seem more real and believable to readers than do ads. Public relations can reach many prospects who avoid salespeople and advertisements — the message gets to the buyers as 'news' rather than as a sales-directed communication. And like advertising, public 5 relations can dramatize a company or product.

2   Marketers tend to underuse public relations or use it as an afterthought. Yet a well-thought-out public relations campaign used with other promotion mix elements can be very effective and economical.

Fig. 4.1   Relative Importance of Promotion Tools in Consumer versus Industrial Markets

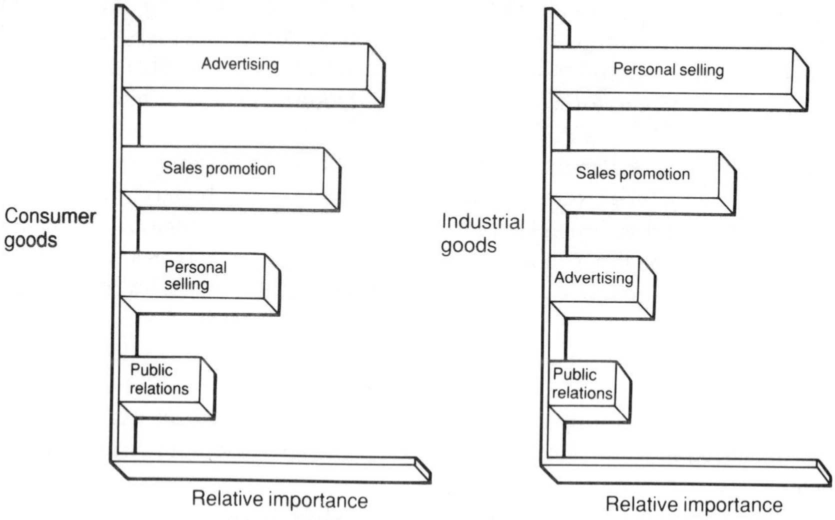

'Marketing' Kotler, P., and Armstrong, G., (Prentice Hall) 2nd Edition

Advertising

1. (a) Which paragraph(s) focus on the good points of advertising?
   (b) What words or expressions in these paragraphs particularly give this impression?

2. (a) Which paragraph(s) focus on the disadvantages of advertising?
   (b) What words and expressions particularly give this impression?

3. Draw up a table summarising the positive and negative features of advertising.

Positive features	Negative features

4. The ideas in this section of the text are very clearly linked using a number of linking expressions.

   (a) Each linking expression in column A could be replaced with an expression from the following box. Choose an expression from the box and write it in column B next to the expression it could replace. (There are more expressions in the box than you need.)

> additionally, due to, in spite of the fact that, moreover, nevertheless, on the other hand, simultaneously, since, therefore.

	Column A	Column B	Column C
because of	line 1		
yet	line 2		
because	line 4		
also	line 6		
although	line 16		
in addition	line 20		

(b) Linking expressions are used in texts to signal that a particular type of information will follow. The box below shows you some types of information.
Match each expression in column A with the type of information it signals. Write the type of information in column C. (Each item can be used more than once.)

> addition, cause, comparison, contrast, reason.

5. (a) 'On the one hand . . . and on the other', lines 11–13, is also a linking expression but with two parts so it signals two types of information. Which pair does it signal in this context?
    (i)   cause and effect
    (ii) addition and contrast
    (iii) fact and explanation
    (iv) comparison and contrast
    (b) Explain the two particular ideas the writer refers to here.

6. Word Relationships: Different endings on the same word-stem change the function of a word. Complete the table below. Some words are in the passage, others you may know or need to look up in a dictionary.

Adjective	Verb	Noun
general	promote	
		standardisation
	legitimise	
	popularise	
	persuade	

Personal selling

7. Look back to the advertising section, activity 3; draw up a similar table listing the positive and negative features of personal selling.

8. (a) Which part of the text deals with positive features?
   (b) How do you recognise when the negative ones are about to be mentioned?

9. (a) What sorts of goods are personal selling most used for?
   (b) Why do you think this is so?

10. Find linking expressions in this section of the passage which can be replaced by the following expressions. Write down the linking expression and the line number.

especially	_____
in comparison to	_____
thus	_____
so as to	_____
even when	_____

Sales promotion

11. (a) Does this section of the passage deal with positive and negative features?
    (b) Do the positive features occur first?
    (c) How are the negative features signalled?

12. (a) Which types of sales promotion does the passage list?
    (b) Can you add to this list?

Public relations

13. (a) What are the positive points for public relations?
    (b) Are any negative points mentioned?

Many of questions 1 to 13 have focused on the author's consistent patterning of information. Question 14 focuses on the content and should provide you with an overall summary.

Summarising

14. (a) What is the main purpose of each category of promotion?
    (b) When would you use each one?

Text 4.2 Premier seeks a premium

Pre-reading:
Where is tea grown?
What do you know about the processing of tea?

Skim and scan:
(a) What is the difference between fresh tea and freshly brewed tea?
(b) 'Typhoo' and 'Premier' are names. Which is a company and which a product?
(c) Who, or what, is Earl Grey?

Premier seeks a premium

Typhoo is exploiting 'fresh tea' flavour

1   Fancy a cup of fresh tea? Not freshly brewed tea, but fresh tea, processed in the normal way but sealed away from air within 24 hours of being
5 picked to prevent loss of flavour.

2   Four out of five people in the UK drink tea, making it the most popular drink apart from tap water, but few of them could imagine what 'fresh tea'
10 entails.

3   That is because Premier Teas, owner of Typhoo, Britain's third largest tea brand, has only just invented the concept — and the
15 product. Premier today will outline to its sales force an ambitious strategy to create a whole new category of one of Britain's most familiar beverages.

4   On the market from February 1,
20 Typhoo Extra Fresh will retail at £1.89 for 80 tea bags compared with £1.49 for the same number of ordinary Typhoo tea bags.

5   Typhoo is faced with the task of
25 persuading consumers that fresh tea really is different, and worth the

premium. As part of advertising and marketing expenditure of £3m, samples will be put through 1.5m letterboxes.   30

6   Premier will tout Typhoo Extra Fresh as 'the first real advance in the quality of tea itself since tea was introduced to the UK in the 17th century'.   35

7   The advertising slogan devised by London consultancy Network Ad Infinitum — 'Not Just Making Tea, Making History' — will reinforce this line.   40

8   Talking about tea at all is unusual in this sector, where advertisers tend to rely on chimps, pursed-lipped actresses oooo...ing or animated 'tea folk' to deliver their message.   45

9   Premier is not counting on a mass switch to Extra Fresh; many drinkers may not like the taste anyway. But it could find a niche as a 'special occasion' tea for drinkers who do not 50 like speciality products like Earl Grey.

'Financial Times' 24 January 1991

Comprehension

1. (a) What is the product being marketed?
   (b) What is different about it?
   (c) What market is anticipated for it?

2. All four categories of promotion are mentioned here. For each one, give the paragraph numbers in which it is mentioned and how it is being used.

Promotional tool	Paragraph number	How it is being used
Advertising Personal Selling Sales Promotion Public Relations		

3. Decide which of the following statements are True or False and give a paragraph number to show where your information came from.

   (a) 'Fresh tea' will be packed within a day of picking.
   (b) Tea is the most popular drink in the UK.
   (c) £3m will be spent on advertising 'fresh tea'.
   (d) Tea was brought to the UK in the 1600s.
   (e) 'Fresh tea' is being produced for the mass market.

Vocabulary

4. Which is the best alternative for the meaning in this passage?

   line 18   beverages   (a) foods
                          (b) teas
                          (c) drinks
                          (d) meals

   line 31   tout   (a) sell unofficially
                          (b) sell more expensively
                          (c) sell door to door
                          (d) sell persuasively

   line 46   genesis   (a) creation
                          (b) coming out
                          (c) growth
                          (d) source

5. What is the 'premium' referred to in paragraph 5?

Unit 5 Pricing

This unit on the price of goods contains four texts. The first discusses the relative importance of pricing while the second outlines ways of setting prices. The third text illustrates one effect of a price change. The final text contains a range of expressions all to do with price.

Text 5.1 Is price all that matters?

Pre-reading:
When you are buying things how often is price very important?
With what sort of goods would you simply choose the cheapest?
When do you buy without caring about the price?

Skim and scan:
(a) What example is given of a substance purchased in bulk?
(b) What does a wise customer do?

Is price all that matters?

1   'Price cutting', it has been said, 'is a technique for slitting someone else's throat and bleeding to death yourself.' Price cutting wars erode profits right across the industry in which they are waged, and are often started by a wholly unnecessary panic reaction to price competition.

2   The view that a competitor's prices must always be matched in order not 5 to lose market share is an unduly pessimistic one, based on the false assumption that the customer is only interested in price.

3   Even in price sensitive industrial commodity markets this is so far from being the case that price is not even the *most* important marketing variable in the eyes of customers. Surveys in the UK and elsewhere have shown that 10 in excess of 60% of DMUs* would not change their best suppliers for a drop in price of 5% plus, and for some the figure would be 10%.

4   Sulphuric acid, for instance, is a bulk commodity that can be described as price sensitive. The large buyer is likely to be involved in running a continuous process. The acid cannot be stored in large quantities, except at 15 prohibitive expense, because it is corrosive, and so if the supply is interrupted for any length of time the customer has to stop production. For this reason he 'multisources' — that is, buys from several suppliers. Even so, supplies

* Decision Making Unit

are far from guaranteed because at peak business periods they will all be stretched. So the wise customer chooses suppliers primarily for reliability, 20 not price.

5   The example demonstrates an important principle: 'The cost to my customer is not necessarily the price I charge.' The customer's costs include the risk of interrupted supply, poor quality, ordering difficulties, and so forth. The buyer's decision, in other words, relates to many more factors than price 25 alone.

6   It follows that knowledge of precisely which factors it is that customers regard as of greatest importance, will enable the marketer to concentrate attention on these points, and steer the buying decision away from price.

'Introducing Marketing' Wills, G., et al (Pan Books) 1984

Text organisation

1. In each paragraph or pair of paragraphs the author has a particular purpose. Match the paragraph numbers with a purpose from the box below.

Paragraphs   Purpose

      1 & 2   _____
        3   _____
        4   _____
        5   _____
        6   _____

Purposes	
stating a principle	giving an example
preparing for the next topic	making a claim
justifying a claim	

Comprehension

2. (a) What is the author's claim:
        (i)   price is not the only issue for buyers
        (ii) a competitor's price must always be matched
        (iii) price wars increase profits
        (iv) price cutting wars are necessary
    (b) What evidence does he quote to justify his claim?

3. (a) Name one substance where a buyer will look for supply reliability.
    (b) Why is supply so important?

4. Buyers will consider a number of factors.

(a) State three which are mentioned in the passage.

(b) Can you suggest any others?

5. Look at the section headings listed below. Which one would follow paragraph 6?

(a) When should price cutting be considered?

(b) Competing on value, not price.

(c) Knowing what the customer values.

(d) When the competition's price is not known.

6. The first sentences of this next section have been jumbled up. What should the order be?

(a) For example, a same-day developing and printing service for film would have a very high value to a short-stay tourist who wished to see how successful his photography had been while he still had the chance to retake the pictures.

(b) This is because products that seem entirely identical to their producers may not rank equally in the eyes of the purchaser.

(c) That same person at home would place a totally different value on such a service.

(d) What the customer regards as important is sometimes far from obvious, and can only be reliably uncovered through detailed market research.

Vocabulary

7. (a) The word 'bulk', line 13 has a number of different meanings. Which meaning does it have in this passage?

bulk /bʌlk/, **bulks, bulking, bulked. 1** A **bulk** is a large mass of something. EG *Willie looked with loathing at the dark bulk of the building.*	N COUNT:USU SING, IF+PREP THEN of
2 A large or fat person's **bulk** is their body. EG *Flora swung her big bulk off the bed . . . Behind her was the unmistakable bulk of Harry Meadows.* ▶ also used to refer to a person's weight or size. EG *For a man of his vast bulk, Gerald had a surprisingly high voice.*	N COUNT: USU SING ▶ N UNCOUNT ⇑ size = proportions
3 The **bulk** of something is most of it. EG *The bulk of his days are spent quietly . . . They constitute the overwhelming bulk of the population.*	N PART:SING = majority
4 If you buy or sell something **in bulk**, you buy or sell it in large quantities, instead of buying or selling it when it has been divided into smaller quantities. EG *They buy food in bulk . . . Goods can be made very much cheaper if they're sold in bulk.*	PHR: USED AS AN A ⇑ in quantity
5 Bulk goods are bought and sold in large quantities. EG *She has a useful list of bulk food suppliers.*	ADJ CLASSIF: ATTRIB
6 If something **bulks large**, it seems very large when you look at it; a literary expression. EG *The Senate House bulked large to the west.*	PHR:VB INFLECTS
bulk buy, bulk buys, bulk buying, bulk bought. If you **bulk buy** goods, you buy them in large quantities in order to save time and money. EG *We live in the city and don't often bulk buy.*	V OR V+O

35

(b) What is another word for 'commodity'?

8. Word Relationships: Complete the following table. As in Unit 2 some of the items are in the text, in paragraphs 3 and 4; others you may know or you may have to use your dictionary.

Verb	Adjective	Noun
supply	X	
sensitise		
		continuation
		prohibition
		corrosion
produce	X	

9. Word Partnerships: Remember often words do not occur on their own but in relationships with certain other words and you will find it more useful to learn pairs or groups of words than individual ones.

For example, in this passage the word 'price' occurs in partnership with several others. What partnerships can you find in the text? What others do you know? Use pages 92–97, at the back of this book to record your examples.

What word partnerships can you find for the word 'cost'? Look also in the texts of previous units.

10. List expressions in this text which are aggressive and establish a violent image.

e.g. lines 2 and 3   to wage war

Text 5.2 Setting the price

Skim and scan:
(a) How many common pricing mistakes are mentioned?
(b) Name two companies which were leaders of the 'one-price' policy.

Setting the Price

1   How are prices set? Through most of history, prices were set by buyers and sellers negotiating with each other. Sellers would ask for a higher price than they expected to receive, and buyers would offer less than they expected to pay. Through bargaining, they would arrive at an acceptable price.

2   Setting one price for all buyers is a relatively modern idea. It was given 5 impetus by the development of large-scale retailing at the end of the nineteenth century. F.W. Woolworth, Tiffany and Co., John Wanamaker, J.L. Hudson, and others advertised a 'strictly one-price policy' because they carried so many items and supervised so many employees.

3 | Through most of history, price has operated as the major determinant of buyer choice. This is still true in poorer nations, among poorer groups, and with commodity-type products. However, nonprice factors have become relatively more important in buyer-choice behavior in recent decades. Yet price still remains one of the most important elements determining company market share and profitability. 10 ... 15

4 | Price is the only element in the marketing mix that produces revenue; the other elements represent costs. Yet many companies do not handle pricing well. The most common mistakes are: pricing is too cost oriented; price is not revised often enough to capitalize on market changes; price is set independently of the rest of the marketing mix rather than as an intrinsic element of market-positioning strategy; and price is not varied enough for different product items and market segments. 20

5 | Companies handle pricing in a variety of ways. In small companies, prices are often set by top management rather than by the marketing or sales department. In large companies, pricing is typically handled by divisional and product-line managers. Even here, top management sets the general pricing objectives and policies and often approves the prices proposed by lower levels of management. In industries where pricing is a key factor (aerospace, railroads, oil companies), companies will often establish a pricing department to set prices or assist others in determining appropriate prices. This department reports either to the marketing department or top management. Others who exert an influence on pricing include sales managers, production managers, finance managers, and accountants. 25 ... 30

'Marketing' Kotler, P., (Prentice Hall)

Comprehension

1. The 'one-price policy' means:

   (a) all items are the same price
   (b) all purchasers pay the same price
   (c) all employees earn the same wage

2. Why did the one-price policy come into existence?
3. What is a major difference between price and the other 3 Ps?
4. Historically, which of the 4 Ps has been most important?
5. Why should prices be reviewed?
6. Complete the summary below by writing **one word** in each gap.

   Nowadays _____ is just one of the factors which influence a would-be _____. While it will always be a consideration, quality, service, reliability, etc. may be equally or even more important considerations. Most _____ are sold at a _____ price, although, particularly with large or repeat orders, some _____ may be feasible. When bargaining a seller expects to _____ the asking price and the buyer expects to _____ the original offer.

   Pricing _____ from the other 3 Ps because it results in _____ while the others all lead to _____. To price well you must continually _____ your price, you must relate it to your market _____ and be prepared to charge _____ _____ in different market segments. In deciding on a price a company should not look only at _____.

Vocabulary

7. Find words in the text with the opposite meaning to those listed below:

	Opposite	Line number
buyers	_____	_____
ancient	_____	_____
small-scale	_____	_____
employers	_____	_____
revenue	_____	_____
extrinsic	_____	_____
fixed	_____	_____

8. What is the meaning of 'yet' (line 13)?

   (a) for a while
   (b) even now
   (c) but

Text 5.3 How price signals product quality

Skim and scan:
  (a) What is the product under discussion?
  (b) How many different strategies did the marketers consider?
  (c) How many different brands does each company have?

How price signals product quality

1   Heublein produces Smirnoff, America's leading brand of vodka. Some years ago, Smirnoff was attacked by another brand, Wolfschmidt, priced at one dollar less per bottle and claiming to have the same quality. Concerned that customers might switch to Wolfschmidt, Heublein considered several possible counterstrategies. It could lower Smirnoff's price by one dollar to hold on 5 to market share; it could hold Smirnoff's price but increase advertising and promotion expenditures; or it could hold Smirnoff's price and let its market share fall. All three strategies would lead to lower profits, and it seemed that Heublein faced a no-win situation.

2   At this point, however, Heublein's marketers thought of a fourth strategy 10 — and it was brilliant. Heublein *raised* the price of Smirnoff by one dollar! The company then introduced a new brand, Relska, to compete with Wolfschmidt. Moreover, it introduced another brand, Popov, priced *lower*

than Wolfschmidt. This product-line pricing strategy positioned Smirnoff as the elite brand and Wolfschmidt as an ordinary brand. Heublein's clever 15 strategy produced a large increase in its overall profits.

3   The irony is that Heublein's three brands are pretty much the same in taste and manufacturing costs. Heublein knew that a product's price signals its quality. Using price as a signal, Heublein sells roughly the same product at three different quality positions.   20

'Marketing Today' Kotler, P., and Armstrong G., (Prentice Hall)

Text organisation

1. As with text 1.3 in Unit 1, the underlying structure of this text is _____ and _____.

2. Complete *part A* of Figure 5.1 below to show the order of information in the text. Select a label for each box from the list below. The first one has been done for you.

positive evaluation	key principle
process	solutions
problem	cause
solution	situation
hypothesis	negative evaluation

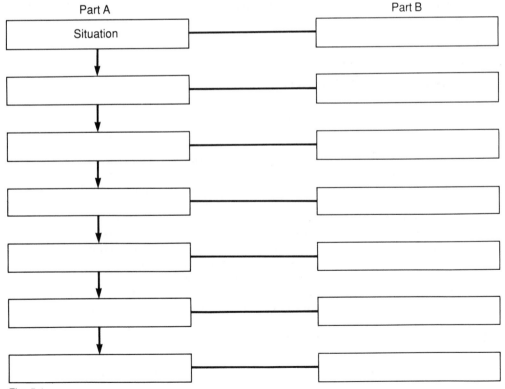

Fig. 5.1

39

Comprehension

3. Decide which of the following are True or False and give a paragraph number to show where your information came from.

   (a) Wolfschmidt said they had produced a vodka that was the same quality as Smirnoff.
   (b) Heublein considered matching Wolfschmidt's price.
   (c) Smirnoff and Relska taste similar.
   (d) The price competition involved physical violence.

4. Return to part B of the chart on page 39. Use it to make notes on the main points.

	PART A		PART B
e.g.:	SITUATION		MARKET FOR VODKA

Viewpoint

5. Do you think it is right for companies to sell very similar products at different prices?

Text 5.4   Price goes by many names

This is a 'fun' text which shows some of the different expressions there are in English for 'price'.

Price goes by many names

1   All profit organizations and many nonprofit organizations face the task of setting a price on their products or services. Price goes by many names:

2   Price is all around us. You pay *rent* for your apartment, *tuition* for your education, and a *fee* to your physician or dentist. The airline, railway, taxi, and bus companies charge you a *fare*; the local utilities call their price a *rate*; and the local bank charges you *interest* for the money you borrow. The price for driving your car on Florida's Sunshine Parkway is a *toll*, and the company that insures your car charges you a *premium*. The guest lecturer charges an *honorarium* to tell you about a government official who took a *bribe* to help a shady character steal *dues* collected by a trade association. Clubs or societies to which you belong may make a special *assessment* to pay unusual expenses. Your regular lawyer may ask for a *retainer* to cover her services. The 'price' of an executive is a *salary*, the price of a salesperson may be a *commission*, and the price of a worker is a *wage*. Finally, although economists would disagree, many of us feel that *income taxes* are the price we pay for the privilege of making money.

'Marketing' Kotler, P., (Prentice Hall)

Vocabulary

1. Make your own table listing price expressions from the text and any others you can think of.

    e.g.:

Verb	Noun phrase
to rent to pay for etc.	an apartment tuition etc.

Unit 6 Marketing services

So far the texts have all dealt with the marketing of goods. An important aspect of the economics of the developed nations is the role of services. Text 1 in this unit considers what services are. Texts 2 and 3 look at some of the features of marketing different services.

Text 6.1 The nature and characteristics of services

Pre-reading:
Which of the following are goods and which are services?

Hospitals   Fast-food outlets   Hamburgers
Sportswear   Sportsclubs   Penicillin

Skim and scan:
(a) How many special characteristics do services have?
(b) What are they?

The nature and characteristics of services

1   Goods are those tangible products that consumers can physically possess. A service is the result of applying human or mechanical efforts to people or objects. Services are intangible products involving a deed, a performance, or an effort that cannot be physically possessed. We should note that few products can be classified as a pure good or a pure service. Consider, for   5 example, an automobile. When consumers purchase a car, they take ownership of a physical item that provides transportation, but the warranty associated with the purchase is a service.

2   The basic concept of services marketing — identical to that of any type of marketing — is to provide customers with benefits that satisfy their needs.   10 In other words, the marketer must develop the right service for the right people at the right price and at the right place. The marketer must also communicate with consumers so that they are aware of the need-satisfying services available to them. Nevertheless, the unique characteristics of services create special problems for a marketing strategy.   15

42

3   The problems of service marketing are not the same as those of goods marketing. To understand these unique problems, it is first necessary to understand the distinguishing characteristics of services. Services have four basic characteristics: (1) intangibility, (2) inseparability of production and consumption, (3) perishability, and (4) heterogeneity. These characteristics 20 and the marketing problems they entail are summarized in Table 6.1.

Table 6.1 *Service characteristics and marketing problems*

Unique service features	Resulting marketing problems
Intangibility	Cannot be stored
	Cannot be protected through patents
	Cannot be readily displayed or communicated
	Prices are difficult to set
Inseparability	Consumer is involved in production
	Other consumers are involved in production
	Centralized mass production is difficult
Perishability	Services cannot be inventoried
Heterogeneity	Standardization and quality are difficult to control

4   **Intangibility** stems from the fact that services are performances. They cannot be seen, touched, tasted, or smelled, nor can they be possessed.

5   Related to intangibility is **inseparability** of production and consumption. Services are normally produced at the same time they are consumed. A medical 25 examination is an example of concurrent production and consumption. In fact, the doctor cannot possibly perform the service without the patient's presence, and the consumer is actually involved in the production process. With other services, such as air travel, many consumers are simultaneously involved in production. Due to high consumer involvement in most services, 30 standardization and control are difficult to maintain.

6   Because production and consumption are simultaneous, services are also characterized by **perishability**. In other words, unused capacity in one time period cannot be stockpiled or inventoried for future time periods. Consider medical examinations again. A doctor may have eight hours per day to see 35 patients. On Monday the doctor may see only two patients for thirty minutes each, leaving seven hours of unused capacity. On Tuesday, the doctor has twenty patients requesting his or her services, each requiring thirty minutes. Since the doctor can see only sixteen patients per day, Tuesday's demand exceeds the doctor's capacity. Unfortunately, the seven hours of excess time 40

7 | on Monday cannot be stockpiled for use on Tuesday when demand is high. This illustrates how service perishability presents problems very different from the supply and demand problems encountered in the marketing of goods.

Finally, because most services are labor intensive, they are susceptible to **heterogeneity**. People typically perform services, and people are not always 45 consistent in their performance. There may be variation from one service to another within the same organization or variation in the service provided by a single individual from day to day and from customer to customer. Thus, standardization and quality are extremely difficult to control.

'Marketing' Pride and Farrell (Houghton Mifflin) 1987

Comprehension

1. Complete the definitions:

   (a) Goods are products which _____ .
   (b) Services are products which _____ .

2. Delete the wrong expression:

   (a) Service and goods marketing have $\left\{ \begin{array}{l} \text{the same} \\ \text{different} \end{array} \right\}$ aims.

   (b) The 4 Ps are important in marketing goods $\left\{ \begin{array}{l} \text{but not} \\ \text{and} \end{array} \right\}$ services.

3. For each situation give one marketing problem and state which one of the four characteristics of services is most dominant.

	Marketing problem	Service characteristic
(a)		
(b)		
(c)		
(d)		

   (a) One airline clerk is quick and cheerful, another is slow and unpleasant.
   (b) A restaurant is fully booked from 8.30 p.m. but has only three customers at 7 p.m.
   (c) When Tina Turner is sick her live show has to be cancelled.
   (d) One dress shop assistant has a particularly good eye for what suits customers.

4. Give a 'goods' aspect and a 'services' aspect for each of the following:

	Goods aspect	Services aspect
automobile meal in a restaurant buying books getting pills from a doctor repairs to a camera		

5. What differences in product and service can you think of between buying bread at a traditional bakery and in a supermarket?

Vocabulary

6. In line 7, 'warranty' means: (a) a warning
                                  (b) written permission
                                  (c) servicing
                                  (d) a guarantee

    In line 14, 'nevertheless' means: (a) because of
                                       (b) however
                                       (c) meanwhile
                                       (d) in fact

    In line 30, 'due to' means: (a) because of
                                 (b) however
                                 (c) meanwhile
                                 (d) in fact

    In Table 6.1, 'patents' means: (a) physical means
                                    (b) laws
                                    (c) official rights
                                    (d) courts

    In Table 6.1, 'inventoried' means: (a) listed
                                        (b) measured
                                        (c) weighed
                                        (d) discovered

7. Which two words in the passage mean 'at the same time'? Fill in the table below; refer to your dictionary if necessary.

	Adverb	Adjective
(a)		
(b)		

Text 6.2 V&A refreshes the arts ...

Pre-reading:
What is the difference between *art* and *the arts*?
What image do museums have for you?
When would you visit a museum?
Can you complete and add to the table below?

Types of arts	Where to see or hear them
Paintings	Concert hall
Drama	

Skim and scan:
(a) What does V&A stand for?
(b) What types of promotion has the V&A used?

Notes: (1) 'An ace caff'
caff = short slang for café; a place to have a drink and inexpensive food
ace = slang for 'first class'

(2) 'V&A refreshes the arts'
An allusion to a famous advertising slogan: 'Heineken refreshes the parts other beers cannot reach'.

V&A refreshes the arts ...

1   Museums and galleries have, some say, been slower to develop marketing skills than their theatrical, orchestral and operatic companions.

2   Most institutions, after all, do not sell tickets to visitors and have been insulated from the commercial pressures of the box office.

3   The Victoria & Albert Museum, however, has proved itself one of the more courageous marketers of recent years.

4   Charles Mills was the museum's first marketing manager, appointed just under three years ago. The V&A boasts it was the first major national museum to have a marketing manager. It was also the first to attempt to charge for entry.

5   Mills was personally responsible for the V&A's much loved and loathed 'Ace Caff' campaign. It ran in 1988, through Saatchi & Saatchi, and is, incidentally, Arts Minister David Mellor's favourite campaign.

6   'That campaign was a milestone,' claims Mills. 'We knew the V&A had a fusty image which was stopping some people visiting us. Trying to shake off this image we produced a campaign that was deliberately controversial.' He adds. 'It had to be controversial to get people talking about it. We had a tiny budget.'

7   'It was certainly provocative,' says Mellor. 'While it had some success raising the profile of the museum, and attracting some new visitors, I suspect it alienated those others for whom the treasures of the museum, rather than its support services, were a main concern.'

8   According to V&A director Elizabeth Esteve-Coll this campaign, combined with a series of strong exhibitions, increased the number of visitors to the V&A by ten per cent in that year.

9   Esteve-Coll wishes she had more money to 'work hard at segments'. She talks about

10

11

12

marketing the V&A's educational appeal and to adult learners, schools and families, among
45 others.

But the museum should congratulate itself that, on its modest budgets, it is beginning to talk to some 'segments' of the population that have previously been outside its
50 traditional visitor profile.

One example is the V&A club, established two years ago. 'The club is every Wednesday evening,' Esteve-Coll explains. 'It was designed for young people who were not coming to
55 the museum during the day because of their work. Now they can come in the evening: the restaurant is open, there is music, and they can bring their friends.'

The new Nehru Gallery of Indian Art opens
60 on November 23. The gallery, containing more than 35,000 objects dating from 1550,

13

14

has been constructed with the help of donations and sponsorship worth £1.7m.

'For the first time we are targeting the Asian community,' says Mills. 'It is our duty to
65 expand our audiences to areas the V&A is not yet attracting. We will be doing mailings to cities in the North where there is a concentration of the Asian community. And for the first time we will be selling the museum
70 through a roadshow, visiting Leicester in December.'

The gallery is also running a cross-track poster campaign, designed in-house, to support the gallery launch. This will be backed
75 by promotions with Indian restaurant Bombay Brasserie, which is creating a new dish to commemorate Nehru's birth. Readers of The Times will also enjoy a promotion.

All right, the chair's a bit weird,
but we don't monkey
around with our dumplings.

 An ace caff with quite a nice museum attached.

Where else do they give you
£100,000,000 worth of objets d'art
free with every egg salad?

An ace caff with quite a nice museum attached.

© V&A

'Marketing Week' 30 November 1990

Comprehension

1. Say whether the following statements are True or False and give the position, e.g. paragraph number(s), where you find the information.

    (a) You have to pay to visit the V&A.
    (b) The V&A café is a support service.
    (c) The V&A markets itself to schools and adult learners.
    (d) The V&A club was started the year after the 'Ace caff' campaign.

2. (a) What did the 'Ace caff' campaign promote?
   (b) How did people react to the 'Ace caff' campaign? Quote from the text to support your answer.

3. Complete the table below:

Promotion technique	Target market
mailings	young working people people in Leicester

   Can you find examples of other techniques in the text?

4. In line 5 'most institutions' refers to _____ .

Viewpoint

5. (a) Does the author of the article approve or disapprove of the V&A's marketing actions?
   (b) Give at least one quotation to justify your answer.

Vocabulary

6. What is the meaning of:

   line 22   milestone   (a) major new step
                         (b) disaster
                         (c) very expensive
                         (d) great success

   line 23   fusty   (a) élite
                     (b) exciting
                     (c) old-fashioned
                     (d) dull

   advertisement 2   dumplings   (a) sculpture
                                 (b) furniture
                                 (c) food
                                 (d) paintings

7. What is a 'box office', line 7?
8. In what way is the heading 'V&A refreshes the arts . . .' a play on words? (Think about the particular aspect of the V&A which was advertised.)

Text 6.3   Person marketing

Pre-reading:
   Can you think of any examples where individuals or groups market themselves?

Skim and scan:
  (a) Is person marketing different to product marketing?
  (b) What is the purpose of person marketing?
  (c) Is it used widely or only by a very few people?

Person marketing

1 People are also marketed. **Person marketing** consists of activities undertaken to create, maintain, or change attitudes or behavior toward particular people. All kinds of people and organizations practise person marketing. Politicians market themselves to get votes and program support. Entertainers and sports figures use 5 marketing to promote their careers and improve their incomes. Professionals such as doctors, lawyers, accountants, and architects market themselves in order to build reputations and increase business. Business leaders use person marketing as a strategic tool to develop their companies' fortunes as well as 10 their own. Businesses, charities, sports teams, fine arts groups, religious groups, and other organizations also use person marketing. Creating, flaunting, or associating with well-known personalities often helps organizations to better achieve their goals. 15

2 Ronald Reagan's presidential administration was unequaled in its use of marketing to sell the president and his policies to the American people. Every move made by Reagan during his eight years as president was carefully managed to support the administration's positioning and marketing strategy. An army 20 of specialists — marketing researchers, advertising experts, political advisers, speech writers, media planners, press secretaries, even make-up artists — worked tirelessly to define political market segments, identify key issues, and strongly position Reagan and his programs. The administration used 25 extensive marketing research. It regularly polled voter segments to find out what was 'hot' and what was not. Using focus groups, it pretested important speeches and platforms. 'Theming it' was an important element of marketing strategy — the administration packaged key benefits into a few highly 30 focused themes, then repeated these basic themes over and over and over. This focus on basic marketable themes, coupled with careful planning and delivery of messages and media exposures, helped control what was reported by the press. Reagan even made careful use of 'regional marketing', tailoring timely 35 speeches to the special needs of regional or local audiences.

3 The objective of person marketing is to create a 'celebrity'

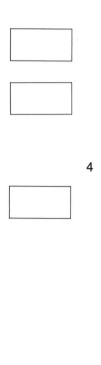

— a well-known person whose name generates attention, interest, and action. Celebrities differ in the *scope* of their visibility. Some are very well known, but only in limited geographic areas (a town mayor, a local businessperson, an area doctor) or specific segments (the president of the American Dental Association, a company vice-president, a jazz musician with a small group of fans). Still others have broad national or international visibility (major entertainers, sports superstars, world political and religious leaders).

4   Celebrities also differ in their *durability*. Figure 6.1 includes a standard celebrity life-cycle pattern. The individual's visibility begins at a low level, gradually builds to a peak as the person matures and becomes well known, then declines as the celebrity fades from the limelight. But as the rest of Figure 6.1 shows, celebrity life-cycle patterns can vary greatly. For example, in the *overnight* pattern a person acquires quick and lasting visibility because of some major deed or event (Charles Lindbergh, Neil Armstrong). In the *comeback* pattern a celebrity achieves high visibility, loses it, then gets it back again (Tina Turner, George Burns). In the *meteor pattern* someone gains fame quickly and then loses it suddenly. For example, William 'Refrigerator' Perry, the overweight Chicago defensive lineman, became an instant 'hot property' after he was used as a running back on Monday Night Football, made millions of dollars from product endorsements, and then sank back into obscurity — all within about a year.

5   The person-marketing process is similar to the one used by product and service marketers. Person marketers begin with careful market research and analysis to discover consumer needs and market segments. Next comes product development — assessing the person's current qualities and image and transforming the person so as to better match market needs and expectations. Finally, the marketer develops programs to value, promote, and deliver the celebrity. Some people naturally possess the skills, appearances, and behaviors that target segments value. But for most, celebrity status in any field must be actively developed through sound person marketing.

'Marketing' Kotler, P., and Armstrong, G., (Prentice Hall) 2nd Edition 1980 & 1987

Text organisation

1. Beside certain paragraphs there are empty boxes. Put the following labels in the correct box; you may use labels more than once.

specific example	definition
general examples	process
specific characteristic	purpose

Comprehension

2. Draw up a table listing: (a) different groups of people who practise person marketing; (b) one or more aim(s) of each group; and (c) an individual example named in the text or based on your own knowledge.

(a) Groups	(b) Aim(s)	(c) An example
e.g. entertainers	promote career increase income	Tina Turner

3. Give three ways in which President Reagan's speeches were fitted to market needs.
4. How was press reporting controlled during Reagan's administration?
5. Graphs A–F in Figure 6.1 do not have captions.

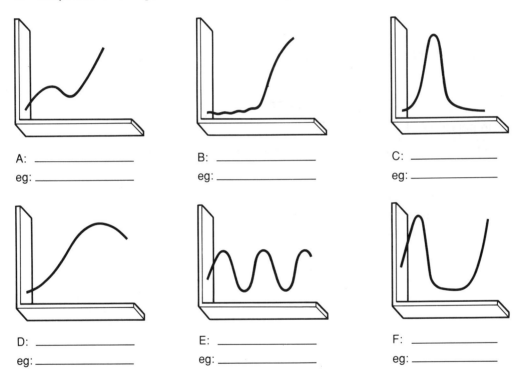

A: _____   B: _____   C: _____
eg: _____   eg: _____   eg: _____

D: _____   E: _____   F: _____
eg: _____   eg: _____   eg: _____

Fig. 6.1   Celebrity Life Cycles

(a) Which of figures A–F represent:

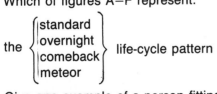

the {standard / overnight / comeback / meteor} life-cycle pattern

(b) Give one example of a person fitting that pattern (from the text or your own knowledge).

51

6. Using the text and your own knowledge can you:

    (a) Give an example of a celebrity with wide scope.
    (b) Give an example of someone with narrow scope.
    (c) Give an example of someone who had wide scope and followed the standard durability pattern.

Vocabulary

7. Using paragraphs 1 and 2 match column A words with their partners in column B.

Column A	Column B
get	support
promote	policies
build	careers
sell	reputations
identify	issues

8. In line 27, 'hot' means: (a) high temperature
                               (b) important
                               (c) difficult
                               (d) popular

9. In paragraph 4

    (a) what expression is used to mean the opposite to: peaks
                                                           gains
                                                           obscurity?
    (b) what word is used as an equivalent in the following?:
        visibility fades or _____
        visibility is acquired or is _____

Unit 7 International marketing

International marketing is an increasingly important topic and in this unit you will read several short texts to give you an idea of what is involved.

Text 7.1 Breaking into an unreceptive market

Pre-reading:
Do you know of countries which restrict the number of goods coming in from foreign countries?

Skim and scan:
(a) When is 'megamarketing' used?
(b) Which company is used as the major example in this text?
(c) How many Ps did this company have to use?

Breaking into an unreceptive market

1   It is one thing to want to do business in a particular country, quite another to be allowed into the country on reasonable terms. The problem of entering an unreceptive or blocked country calls for *megamarketing* — using economic, psychological, political, and public relations skills to gain the cooperation of several parties in the country.   5

2   For example, Pepsi-Cola used megamarketing in its attempt to enter the huge India market. Pepsi worked with an Indian business group to seek government approval for its entry. Both domestic soft-drink companies and anti-multinational legislators objected to letting Pepsi in, so Pepsi had to make an offer that the Indian government would find hard to refuse. It thus offered 10 to help India export enough of its agricultural products to more than offset the outlay for importing soft-drink syrup. Pepsi also promised to focus a good deal of selling effort on rural areas to help in their economic development. The company further offered to give food-processing, packaging, and water-treatment technology to India.   15

3   Clearly, Pepsi's strategy was to bundle a set of benefits that would win the support of the various interest groups influencing the entry decision. Pepsi's marketing problem was not one of simply applying the four *P*'s in a new market, but rather one of just getting into the market in the first place. In trying to win over the government and public groups — and to maintain 20

53

4 | a reasonable relationship once admitted — Pepsi had to add two more *P*'s: 'politics' and 'public opinion'.

Many other large companies have learned that it pays to build good relations with host governments. Olivetti, for example, enters new markets by building housing for workers, supporting local arts and charities, and 25 hiring and training local managers. IBM sponsors nutrition programs for Latin American children and gives agricultural advice to the Mexican government. Polaroid is helping Italy restore Leonardo da Vinci's *Last Supper*.

Sources: See Philip Kotler, 'Megamarketing', *Harvard Business Review*, March–April 1986, pp. 117–24; Kenneth Labich, 'America's International Winners', *Fortune*, April 14, 1986, p. 46; and Sheila Tefft, 'The Mouse That Roared at Pepsi', *Business Week*, September 7, 1987, p. 42.

'Marketing' Kotler, P., and Armstrong, G., (Prentice Hall) 2nd Edition 1980 & 1987

Comprehension

1. When Pepsi wanted to sell goods in India:

   (a) Who did Pepsi work with?
   (b) Who did not want Pepsi products in their country?
   (c) Who did Pepsi make agreements with?
   (d) What was Pepsi's main problem?

2. (a) In how many main areas did Pepsi offer help to India?
   (b) How does the writer signal this in the text?

3. What are the Ps of megamarketing?

4. Fill in the table below to summarise the megamarketing techniques of the companies mentioned.

Company	Product	Special strategies
1. Pepsi		1. 2. 3.
2.		1. 2. 3.
3.		1. 2.
4.		1.

Vocabulary

5. (a) What does 'mega' mean?
   (b) What do the following mean?:
       (i) megamarketing
       (ii) megaphone
       (iii) megalomania

6. (a) Look in the passage to find the verbs that complete the expressions below:

_____ the cooperation of
_____ approval for
_____ an offer
_____ the outlay
_____ the support of
_____ good relations

(b) Which two of these verbs are interchangeable?
(c) What is the difference in meaning between: 'to seek the support of' and 'to win the support of'?
(d) What verbs would make the expressions mean the opposite?

Text 7.2 The world's champion marketers: the Japanese?

Pre-reading:
What Japanese goods do you know?

Skim and scan:
(a) Where did the Japanese learn about marketing?
(b) What four aspects did they learn?
(c) Name four American companies that have marketed successfully in Japan.

The world's champion marketers: the Japanese?

1 | Few dispute that the Japanese have performed an economic miracle since World War II. In a very short time, they have achieved global market leadership in many industries: automobiles, motorcycles, watches, cameras, optical instruments, steel, shipbuilding, computers, and consumer electronics. They are now making strong inroads into tires, chemicals, machine tools, 5 and even designer clothes, cosmetics, and food. Some credit the global success of Japanese companies to their unique business and management practices. Others point to the help they get from Japan's government, powerful trading companies, and banks. Still others say Japan's success is based on low wage rates and unfair dumping policies. 10

2 | In any case, one of the main keys to Japan's success is certainly its skillful use of marketing. The Japanese came to the United States to study marketing and went home understanding it better than many U.S. companies do. They know how to select a market, enter it in the right way, build market share, and protect that share against competitors. 15

3   *Selecting Markets.* The Japanese work hard to identify attractive global markets. First, they look for industries that require high skills and high labor intensity but few natural resources. These include consumer electronics, cameras, watches, motorcycles, and pharmaceuticals. Second, they like markets in which consumers around the world would be willing to buy the same product designs. Finally, they look for industries in which market leaders are weak or complacent.

4   *Entering Markets.* Japanese study teams spend several months evaluating a target market, searching for market niches that are not being satisfied. Sometimes they start with a low-priced, stripped-down version of a product, sometimes with a product that is as good as the competition's but priced lower, sometimes with a product with higher quality or new features. The Japanese also line up good distribution channels in order to provide quick service. They also use effective advertising to bring products to the consumer's attention. Their basic entry strategy is to build market share rather than early profits: The Japanese are often willing to wait as long as a decade before realizing their profits.

5   *Building Market Share.* Once Japanese firms gain a market foothold, they begin to expand market share. They pour money into product improvements and new models so that they can offer more and better products than the competition. They spot new opportunities through market segmentation, develop markets in new countries, and work to build a network of world markets and production locations.

6   *Protecting Market Share.* Once the Japanese achieve market leadership, they become defenders rather than attackers. Their defense strategy is continuous product development and refined market segmentation.

7   U.S. firms are now fighting back by adding new product lines, pricing more aggressively, streamlining production, buying or making components abroad, and forming strategic partnerships with foreign companies. Moreover, many U.S. companies are now operating successfully in Japan itself. American companies sell over 50,000 different products in Japan, and many hold leading market shares — Coke leads in soft drinks (60 percent share), Schick in razors (71 percent), Polaroid in instant cameras (66 percent), and McDonald's in fast food. Since the early 1980s, U.S. companies have increased their Japanese computer sales by 48 percent, pharmaceutical sales by 41 percent, and electronic parts sales by 63 percent.

Sources: See Philip Kotler, Liam Fahey, and Somkid Jatusripitak, *The New Competition* (Englewood Cliffs, NJ: Prentice Hall, 1985); Vernon R. Alden, 'Who Says You Can't Crack Japanese Markets?' *Harvard Business Review*, January–February 1987, pp. 52–56; and Joel Dreyfuss, 'How to Beat the Japanese at Home', *Fortune*, August 31, 1987, pp. 80–83.

'Marketing' Kotler, P., and Armstrong, G., (Prentice Hall) 2nd Edition 1980 & 1987

Comprehension

1. (a) What reason does the author give for Japan's success?
   (b) How many other reasons are mentioned?
   (c) Which words make it clear that these are not the author's explanations?

2. (a) How many strategies are US firms using to combat Japan's influence?
   (b) What are these?

3. Which goods are mentioned as products for both the US and Japan?

4. Summarise Japan's marketing strategy by completing the notes below:

   Selecting markets
   The three sets of features that the Japanese look for are: _____ .

   Entering markets
   The three main actions:

	Action	Purpose
1.		
2.		
3.		

   Main strategy =

   Building market share
   The three main strategies are: _____ .

   Protecting market share
   There are two main strategies: _____ .

Vocabulary

5. Explain these expressions from the text:

   line 5   making strong inroads into
   line 10   unfair dumping policies
   line 25   stripped-down version
   line 34   pour money into

6. Scan through the text to find a verb that completes the following expressions:

   paragraph 4: to _____ distribution channels
               to _____ profits
   paragraph 7: to _____ production

Text 7.3 Heinzight

Pre-reading:
What Heinz products can you name?
What do 'foresight' and 'hindsight' mean?
What do you think the passage title is meant to mean?
What does the expression 'spill the beans' mean?
What was the significance of 1992 for Europe?

Skim and scan:
(a) Which area of the world is focused on in this passage?
(b) In which country does Heinz have the largest sales?
(c) What is Paul Corddry's job?
(d) A survey was conducted; how many companies were involved?

Heinzight

Wanting to turn a brand into a European leader, and making it happen are two different things. To do so, Heinz has had a structural overhaul. Tom Lester spills the beans

1 Heinz is one of the few food companies in the world that really deserves the description 'successful'. It wasn't the sort of company which became the subject of stock market crazes and over-the-top press eulogies, only for everything to fall apart a couple of years later. Its record is consistent. Last year, it celebrated 25 years of unbroken profit growth.

2 But Heinz has a problem. In the UK its brand franchise in such staples as baked beans, ketchups and soups is unassailable. But the UK's 1989 turnover of around £430m represents more than its sales in the rest of Europe put together. Italy, the next largest subsidiary, is about one third the size.

3 Not surprisingly, for years Heinz's UK marketers could sensibly ignore the company's continental operations. After all, the Continentals find the idea of beans in a tomato sauce out of a tin quite bizarre. But in a market where other companies are increasingly thinking in European terms such an attitude begins to represent a dangerous long-term weakness. In the key markets of France and Germany Heinz's market penetration is too low for comfort. Competitors would move in on potential and existing markets and opportunities for expansion would be lost.

4 Two years of rethinking and a McKinsey management consultant report later, and Paul Corddry, who heads the multinational food company's operations in Europe, claims things are different now. When he picks up a bottle of ketchup and says he wants to make it a European brand leader, he means it. Making it happen is a different matter.

5 Corddry's problem has hardly been unique. Virtually every major company has had to sit down and review its product range, potential and marketing priorities in the light of 1992, only to discover that the really difficult bit is the task of overhauling and restructuring the company itself, including its marketing operations, to fit the new priorities. After all, seeing new opportunities and thinking up ways of seizing them is what marketers like doing. Rethinking company structure, redrawing lines of responsibility and breaking down long-established empires and prerogatives are a different matter.

6 According to a new report out this month, this problem has been exercising most companies. Well over half the 40 companies questioned had made major changes in their structures in the past two years. Some, like Lego or Gillette, which rule from the centre, have started giving local operating units more flexibility.

7 Others, like Nestlé or Electrolux, which adopted a decentralised approach in the past, have found themselves doing the opposite. Indeed, the distinction between the two structures and cultures has become increasingly blurred. And often it has been a painful process. Persuading senior managers in each country to think on a European scale, or even to co-operate informally with opposite numbers, has been a real problem.

'Marketing' November 1990

Comprehension

1. Decide which of the following statements are True or False and give a paragraph number to show where your information came from.

   (a) For a quarter of a century Heinz has not made a loss.
   (b) Heinz's sales in Italy are about £1290m.
   (c) Heinz is satisfied with its sales in Germany.
   (d) Other companies have similar problems to Heinz.
   (e) Forty companies have changed their structure.

2. (a) What marketing problem did companies think they had for 1992?
   (b) What did they find was the real problem?
   (c) What solutions have they put into operation?
   (d) What has been a consequence of that?

Text organisation

3. Does the text

   (a) move from General to Particular or Particular to General?
   (b) give good news and then bad news or bad news and then good news?
   (c) mention a problem/need and then a solution or a solution and then the problem/need?

Vocabulary

4. (a) Re as a prefix means _____
   (b) List all the words in the text with this prefix and give their meaning.

5. Which meaning does 'staple' (line 11) have in this text?

staple /stɛɪpəl/, **staples, stapling, stapled. 1** A **staple** is **1.1** a small piece of wire used for holding sheets of paper together firmly. You push the staple through the sheets of paper using a special device called a stapler. **1.2** a U-shaped piece of stiff wire used for holding things in place. Its ends are pushed into wood or brick by using a hammer or other tool.	N COUNT ⇑ clip N COUNT ⇑ fastener
2 If you **staple** something, you fasten it to something else or fix it in place using staples. EG *The letter was stapled to the other documents in the file . . . Various notices had been stapled on the board.*	V+O+A
3 A **staple** meal or food is one that forms a regular and basic part of your everyday life. EG *. . . their staple meals of fish and rice.* **4** A **staple** is also **4.1** a type of food or crop that forms a regular and basic part of the diet of a group of people or of a species of animal. EG *Insects are a staple for most frogs.* **4.2** an important product in a particular region or in a particular industry. EG *Cloth is still a main staple of business in this part of Soho . . . Prices for staples came down in real terms.*	ADJ CLASSIF: ATTRIB ⇐ normal = standard N COUNT = necessity, essential N COUNT = mainstay

4.3 something that forms an important or regular part of   N COUNT
something else. EG *The theme of insanity has recently become
a staple in drama and film.*

6. (a) Find two expressions in this passage which use the concept of 'height'.
   (b) Explain what they mean.

7. Word Partnerships: In texts 7.1, 7.2 and 7.3 there are at least twenty-five instances
   when the word 'market' or 'marketing' is used as part of a partnership. Go through
   each text and add to your partnership lists on pages 92—97. Try to find ways to
   group them to help you remember them.

Unit 8 Marketing and society

There are some concerns regarding the marketing of certain goods and their impact on society. Clearly these are issues where different viewpoints are possible. The articles in this unit present some of these viewpoints.

Text 8.1 Societal marketing

Skim and scan:
   (a) How many definitions of marketing are given?
   (b) Do they differ from those in the first two units?
   (c) When was the 'societal marketing concept' introduced?
   (d) When was the marketing concept born in the West?

Societal marketing

1   Marketing is generally conceived of as human activity directed at satisfying needs and wants through exchange processes (Kotler, 1984) or 'a process of exchange between individuals and/or organisations which is concluded to the mutual benefit and satisfaction of the parties' (Baker, 1983, p.4). Despite being an extremely old activity, dating from times of trade by barter, it is only since the 1950s that marketing has been recognised in the West as an orientation for business activity. In that decade the marketing concept was born.

2   The marketing concept was widely embraced over the next 20 years in Western conditions of rapid economic growth, greater affluence, important inventions, increased competition, narrower profit margins and planned obsolescence. Today some critics have called the concept inadequate and dangerous since it focuses on demand without sufficiently considering such wider issues as scarcity, environmental destruction, inflation and explosive population growth. In response the societal marketing concept has been suggested (Kotler, 1984), which means that the company must consider the welfare of society as a whole as well as satisfying consumer needs and wants.

'Marketing in/for Developing Countries' Kinsey (Prentice Hall)

Comprehension

1.   How does the societal marketing concept differ from the marketing concept?
2.   What are the criticisms levelled at the marketing concept?

Vocabulary

3. 'rapid economic growth', line 10, and 'explosive economic growth', lines 14–15, both mean very fast. What extra meaning does 'explosive' give to the expression?

Texts 8.2 and 8.3

The two texts deal with the same topic so there are some exercises requiring information from both texts and some where the information is in just one of the texts.

Pre-reading:
Recycling has become an important 'green' issue. What is recycling?
What goods can you think of that are recycled?
How are they or their components used?

Skim and scan:
Fill in the table below using information in the texts:

	Company	Good(s) produced	Material(s) used in manufacture
Text 8.2			
Text 8.3			

Text 8.2   Old cars get a new lease of life

Old cars get a new lease of life

1   By the middle of this year BMW and other German vehicle manufacturers will be setting out proposals to the Bonn government on how best to
5   tackle the pressing problem of recycling cars.

2   The German automobile industry has spent more than DM 500m (£170m) on production-related
10   environmental protection over the past few years — equivalent to DM 300 per vehicle in the home market, according to BMW.

3   But the new focus on recycling the
15   2m cars scrapped annually in west Germany alone is not wholly the result

of the manufacturers wishing to be seen to reduce the car's adverse impact on the environment and the resources required in its production.

They are preparing, instead, for the introduction of legislation which will impose tighter controls on the dumping of cars. The legislation may even force manufacturers to take back scrap cars which came off their own production lines. By the end of 1993 manufacturers are likely to be required to have in place the facilities and procedures for such recycling to take place.

It is partly with the aim of achieving that goal that Germany's first pilot car recycling plant has come on stream at BMW's Landshut components plant, less than an hour's drive from Munich.

The recycling centre is on a smaller scale than the 250,000 units-a-year facility BMW would need if it were to recycle all its own output of cars sold inside German borders — and which is already in the outline planning stages.

At any one time workers inside the plant are dismantling cars in their entirety — a task which takes some four to five hours per vehicle.

Horst-Henning Wolf, the recycling project leader, expects the exercise to reveal the most efficient techniques for disassembling cars and, in the longer term, important information about how cars of the future might best be designed in order to recycle them completely, compared with the 75 per cent level which has already been achieved.

As part of the process, BMW hopes to produce cars in such a way that complete disassembly can be cut to about one hour. Landshut has six stages: doors, boots and bonnets; the interior; inside the boot; outer bodywork; engine compartment; and floor pan.

BMW is using what Wolf describes as a 'cascade' concept in its approach to recycling. This means choosing materials which, if possible, are reusable; designing the car to be capable of maximum disassembly; using materials which contain no harmful substances; using as few different materials as possible (in future avoiding materials such as polyvinylchloride and duromers which are problematic to dispose of as well as metal/plastic combinations in a single component); developing a uniform system of plastic marking, so that each can be instantly identified and processed appropriately; and reconditioning as many parts as possible so that they may be re-used.

Some of the processes by which this is achieved have long been familiar. Landshut, for instance, reconditions 16,000 engines a year, 8,000 rear axles and 13,000 starter motors. In the pilot recycling plant, one operation is devoted to extracting from defunct exhaust systems catalytic converter cores with their precious metal coatings. BMW is already reclaiming 8,500 a year. Because more than 80 per cent of all of the precious metals can be recovered, each reclaimed 'cat' is worth DM300–DM400. Lights and water pumps are also reconditioned and re-sold.

Other processes are newer. BMW is collaborating with a number of companies on high-temperature gasification of problematical waste such as oil, rubber and contaminated plastics. A paper mill, for example, is changing its furnace from being coal-fired to using automotive waste. Such furnaces offer potential for the recycling of tyres — millions of which are occupying landfill sites the world over.

The variety of materials found in vehicles makes the recycling problem a complex one. Apart from steel,

14

plastics and rubber, all the fluids used in a vehicle from battery acid to brake fluid are involved, together with glass, 120 leather, wood and electronic parts.

The pilot Landshut project, which will run for two years, is also compiling data on the time and expense involved in disassembly and 125 the extent to which costs can be recouped in the form of direct sales of old parts and recycled materials. The list of potential buyers is surprisingly long.

15

According to Wolf, those lining up 130 to buy recycled BMWs include raw materials producers, the cement, rubber, plastic and mineral oil industries, tyre and glass manufacturers, energy suppliers, the chemical in- 135 dustry and even road construction companies wishing to use granulated plastics which cannot be melted down for re-use as filler in road beds.

'Financial Times' 3 April 1991

Comprehension

1. Say whether the following statements are True or False and give the position e.g. paragraph number(s), to show where your information came from.

    (a) 2m cars are produced each year in Germany.
    (b) BMW may have to recycle a quarter of a million cars a year.
    (c) It is expected that three-quarters of each car will be recyclable.
    (d) Exhaust systems are reconditioned and re-sold.
    (e) Tyres can be converted into fuel.
    (f) The Landshut project will last for two years.
    (g) Some car parts are recycled for use in road building.

2. Complete the following by writing a few words in each gap.

    The two main aims of the Landshut pilot are first to learn _____ and then to learn _____ _____ .

3. Which of the following are part of the cascade effect?

    Using non-toxic materials
    Using many different materials
    Combining metal and plastic

    Selecting recyclable materials
    Marking metal components
    Identification scheme for plastics

Text 8.3   Reincarnation in the design studio

Reincarnation in the design studio

German companies have led the way in the design of energy-efficient products, including appliances and automobiles. **Andrew Fisher** examines AEG's cradle-to-grave approach.

1 In the days when life was simpler, a washing machine was an object which could be used for 10 years or more — maybe 20 if you were lucky — and then discarded for a new one. No one bothered much about what happened to the old machine. You might get something for the scrap value, or have to pay someone to take it away.

2 Gradually, as consumers became aware of the costs and risks of uncontrolled energy use, more emphasis was put on the machine's efficiency during its life span. Today, appliances use far less water and electricity than their predecessors; detergents, too, have become phosphate free and thus less ecologically suspect.

3 German companies such as Miele, Siemens-Bosch and AEG are now at the threshold of another, potentially far-reaching development: the design and manufacture of machines which can be recycled easily at the end of their life.

4 This is not as easy as it may sound. Apart from the volume and variety of materials involved, there is the problem of evaluating their recycling properties. Not enough data are available for this at present and designers are not trained to do this anyway.

5 But at a time when waste disposal is becoming an increasingly acute social, economic, and political issue, the design of washing machines and other appliances in a way that prevents them from becoming an environmental burden later is being given intensive study.

6 'The avoidance of waste is the most serious challenge we are facing today,' says Peter Riller, AEG's director of washing machine and dishwasher design. 'This makes it necessary to equip appliances with an increased number of reusable components'.

7 AEG began taking account of the whole cradle-to-grave life-cycle of washing machines three years ago. 'We are only at the beginning,' Riller says, 'the map is still blank.' He finds the idea of integrating the machine's development and manufacture with the ecology a fascinating one.

8 It means AEG's own people have to be imbued with a greater environmental awareness, not just as citizens but also as employees. Suppliers have to learn more about the recycling qualities of their materials and consumers must gradually accept that the products they buy should be geared towards easier scrapping and reuse of their contents.

9 For example, most Europeans who buy appliances like the look of shiny steel, especially if they are paying a lot of money. But greater use of plastics — as in Japan — could increase efficiency by reducing weight, and eventually lead to improvements in recyclability.

10 Riller reckons that the plastics content of machines could be raised to 10 or 15 per cent from the present 5 per cent. Plastics recycling is still at the early stages of development, however, and until proper recycling concepts are introduced AEG plans no significant increase in plastics use.

11 There is no point, he says, in more so-called downcycling, in which recycling leads to lower grade plastics which are only good for plant pots. The market for these is not infinite. Processes must be developed in which plastics can be recycled so they can be used again for the same or similar applications. 'If we succeed in doing this, the logical next step would be to develop highly plastic machines as the only way of achieving a better overall ecological balance.'

12 Three problems must be solved:

13 • Plastics must be produced so that once the appliance's life is over they are not irreversibly damaged and can thus be recycled or reused.

• Products must consist of a limited number of plastics, the ideal being only one type. At AEG, polypropylene, with especially good anti-corrosion and air-resistant properties, accounts for 70 per cent of the plastics in washing machines, and this proportion will be raised.

• Ways must be found of recovering plastics from the appliances efficiently and without damage.

AEG's research unit is making studies of materials' recycling properties, and the company is also co-operating with outside institutes. With other German manufacturers and companies involved in recycling such as Metallgesellschaft, AEG is also co-operating with the German Electrical Industry Association (ZVEI) on plastics recovery and reuse.

Riller heads a ZVEI working party on the disposal of used appliances and packaging. 'Too many machines still end up on waste dumps,' says Norbert Knaup, general manager of ZVEI's large electrical appliance division.

Chemical, steel, and engineering companies are all working on ways of recycling plastics. While the subject is still under study, ZVEI wants appliance makers to refrain from trying to gain any advantage through advertising their products' recycling qualities. 'The whole matter is too serious to be made into a competitive theme,' Knaup feels.

Three years ago, AEG began marking plastic parts to make identification easier when the appliance's life was over. It also instals components which contain compounds in such a way that these can be easily separated out later.

But real progress will not come until recycling methods have been developed for plastics which are as effective as those for metals, which are first pulverised and then separated mechanically.

Since washing machines run for at least a decade, it will not be until the next century that the results of the work by AEG and others on recyclable appliances can be seen.

The machines of the future will not just wash clothes; they will be part of a whole new approach to keeping the environment clean. No wonder Riller talks of fascinating times ahead.

WHITE GOODS

Reduction in energy use since 1970

Reduction in water use since 1980

Energy used in manufacture and 10-year use of a washing machine

Source: AEG

8000kWh

PRODUCTION

6000kWh

USE

4000kWh

2000kWh

55%

48%

55%

40%

38%

33%

Washing machines

Freezers

Refrigerators

Dishwashers

Source: AEG, Electrical Industry Association (ZVEI)

1970 1989

'Financial Times' 3 April 1991

Comprehension

1. Peter Riller says three groups of people will be affected by the need to produce and market recyclable washing machines. Name the three groups of people and say what change they will need to make.

	Group	Change needed
(a) (b) (c)		

2. (a) What is 'downcycling'?
   (b) Why is its application limited?

3. (a) Are the recyclable qualities of goods used in advertising?
   (b) Why is this?

4. Complete the following statements by writing one word in each gap:

   (a) Modern washing machines use about ____ per cent _____ energy than in _____.
   (b) There has been a _____ increase in the efficiency of dishwashers than in the efficiency of washing machines. Likewise _____ have ____ improved as much as _____.
   (c) Washing machines manufactured in _____ contain a higher proportion of plastics than those manufactured in _____.

Vocabulary

5. There are a number of two-word expressions used in the text. Match the word on the left with one on the right and check you understand the meaning of the expression you make. (They all occur in paragraphs 1–8 of the text.)

   scrap   disposal
   life   components
   phosphate   value
   waste   awareness
   environmental   span
   reusable   free

Combined questions

Use both Text 8.2 and 8.3 to answer these questions.

1. In which paragraph is the theme of 'recycling' first mentioned in:

   Text 8.2 _____
   Text 8.3 _____

2. What is Text 8.3's other theme?
3. When is that theme first mentioned?
4. Where is there more information on this topic?
5. Say whether the following statements are True or False and give the position, e.g. paragraph numbers from both texts, where you find the information.

   (a) AEG and BMW have identification schemes for plastics.
   (b) AEG and BMW are aiming to use just one type of plastic in their products.
   (c) There is more recycling from cars than from washing machines.

6. Complete the summary by writing one word in each gap.

   Recycling is being addressed seriously in _____ because of social and economic pressure but also because of new _____ that has been and is likely to be introduced. For example, it is probable that, by _____, _____ manufacturers will have to _____ all the scrapped _____ that originated on their production lines.
       BMW has built a pilot recycling _____ in which scrapped cars are _____. Currently this takes about _____ or _____ hours but the aim is to design new cars so that this can be achieved in about _____ _____. A number of parts have been recycled for many years, particularly _____ based ones and recently _____ has been introduced for oil, rubber, etc.
       A major problem remains with _____ where recycling is less well developed. As well as devising new processes so that the highgrade material can be recycled without _____, companies, such as _____ and _____, are looking at new _____ features. Goods will need to be designed so that they contain just one or a very limited number of different plastics and in such a way that the _____ can be extracted without damage. While data is expected from the car recycling plant in just _____ years it will take at least _____ for washing machine manufacturers to achieve results.

7. What aspects of societal marketing do these two examples address?

Text 8.4 No smoke without brand fire

Pre-reading:
   What are some of the attitudes to smoking in your country?
   Are there any restrictions on advertising cigarettes, etc.?
   What are some of the arguments anti-smokers use?
   What does the saying 'No smoke without fire' mean?

Skim and scan:
   (a) What is the writer's main marketing point?
   (b) What does the writer consider as the real principle underlying the issue of tobacco promotion?

No smoke without brand fire

1
There is a lot of nonsense being spouted about the issue of tobacco promotion. On the one hand there are those who see it as an issue of principle — as long as tobacco is legally on sale, it should be provided 'freedom of commercial speech'.

2
This is absurd. It picks a fight on the worst possible grounds (a product that 'kills') and it sidesteps the real issue, which is not the principle of advertising regulation, but what sort of restrictions should apply.

3
On the other side, and equally absurd, are those who see the banning of tobacco advertising (and perhaps, sponsorship) as the be all and end all of their campaign. It is utter nonsense to think that Silk Cut and Marlboro would stop selling if all advertising was banned. The brands are far too powerful.

4
Which gets us to the real point: the power of branding, as opposed to mere advertising. Anyone serious about being anti-tobacco would use all the 'P's to undermine cigarette brands, just as marketers use all the 'P's to build them.

5
The Product could be made less appealing and less dangerous by making it smaller. They would look less elegant and 20 a day would mean less tobacco.

6
Legislation on packaging could really undermine cigarette brands. What would happen if manufacturers were forced to sell their goods in packs without logo, called perhaps, '20 Govt standard, Type A, Low Tar'?

7
Then there's Price. How about putting up the price to pay for a powerful anti-smoking campaign? The sponsorship problem would disappear. Few manufacturers would want to sponsor the 'Imperial Type B Snooker Championships'.

8
And how about Place? Ban cigarette sales from everywhere but CTNs*, and extend the current bans on smoking in public places. Add all these together, and the hotly debated 'principles' paraded about tobacco advertising would all but disappear — and the real principle, a political decision about society's attitude towards the product, would come to the fore.

9
The point of all this? First, to show that those who really want to tackle an issue such as tobacco should think in terms of marketing, rather than advertising.

10
Second, to point out how ignorance of the real power of marketing is muddying the waters. Finally, and most important of all to emphasise to all those doubters, in the boardroom and out, just how powerful the full marketing mix is. Under-estimate it at your peril.

* Confectioners, Tobacconists and Newsagents

'Marketing' 28 February 1991

Comprehension

1. There are pro- and anti-advertising tobacco groups.
    In the table below

    (a) fill in each group's reason or belief
    (b) fill in the weakness the writer mentions for each of these

	For tobacco advertising	Against tobacco advertising
Reason/ belief Weakness		

2. Summarise the author's 'demarketing' of cigarettes by completing the table below. List the suggested actions and then the expected results of those actions.

	Price	Product	Place	Promotion
Action				
Result of action			—	

3. Take a product you dislike or disapprove of and suggest a 'Demarketing Plan' for it. Use a table like the one above.

Answer key

Unit 1 Marketing concepts

Text 1.1

Skim and scan
(a) paragraph 2
(b) food, warmth, shelter

Text organisation
1. pargraph 1: What marketing is not
   paragraph 2: What marketing is
   paragraph 3: Reasons for marketing

Comprehension
2. (a) T, paragraph 1
   (b) F, paragraph 1
   (c) F, paragraph 2
   (d) T, paragraph 3

3. Marketing is a process by which
   people/humans obtain what they need
   and want by exchanging goods or
   services.

Text 1.2

Skim and scan
(a) 4
(b) products and/or financial
    resources
(c) The 4 Ps: creation = product,
    distribution = place, price and
    promotion.

Comprehension
1. (a) Definition 2: humans/people
       Definition 3: individual and
       organizational activity
   (b) Definition 2: goods or services
       Definition 3: goods, services and
       ideas
   (c) distribution, promotion and pricing

2. (i) participation
   (ii) possession of something of value
   (iii) willingness to exchange
   (iv) communication

3.

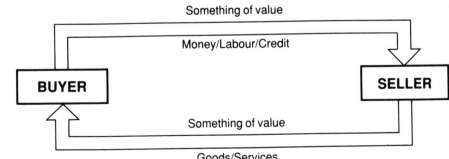

71

4. facilitate = make something easier
   expedite = make something happen faster

5. (a) (i) product
      (ii) place or position
   (b)

Text 1.3

Skim and scan
1. = (b)

Text organisation
1. (a) early 1980s (by the mid-1980s)
   (b) concentration on production instead of selling, i.e. a failure of marketing.
   (c) no growth (static sales)
   (d) mid-1980s
   (e) (i) stopping production at some distilleries
       (ii) writing off of stocks
       (iii) strong marketing
   (f) market strongly (to concentrate on selling versus production)

Comprehension
2. (a) price, place and product brands
   (b) place
   (c) promotion

Vocabulary
3. Johnnie Walker, Mars, Coca Cola, i.e. those associated with a specific product or range of products.

4. hanging over: existing or causing a problem (definition 1)
   going nowhere: constant, static (definition 4)
   doldrums: inactive, static
   mothballing: keep without actively using
   lake: large quantity
   writing off: gave up trying to sell it (definition 2)

Text comparison

1. & 2.

	Text 1.1	Text 1.2	Text 1.3
Source	student textbook	student textbook	newspaper
Typical features	definitions use of 'we', 'our lives'	definitions formal vocabulary	short paragraphs colourful vocabulary informal vocabulary

Unit 2 Products

Text 2.1

Skim and scan

(a) customers buy benefits not products
(b) because technology and development can lead to better ways of achieving the benefit
(c) narrow vision; confusing products with markets

Comprehension

1. Table A

		Products	Benefits
Paragraph 2	(a) floor polish (b) insurance policy (c) Ferraris (d) cutting oil	clean floors security status, high performance engines lubrication	
Additional e.g.	new abrasive disc calculator	time-saving cost-effective computing sums quickly	

2. (a) 'those few words' = 'customers don't buy products: they seek to acquire benefits'.
   (b) 'the result' = of investing time and money
   (c) 'this' = the new disc

Vocabulary
3. maxim = (b)
    pass it by = (a)
    lip service = (c)
4. simultaneously = at the same time
                       (line 22)
    longstanding = traditional (line 23)
    out of date = obsolete (line 30)

includes = incorporates (line 35)
careful to avoid = on guard against
                   (line 37)
mixing up = confusing (line 39)
ongoing = dynamic (line 40)

Text 2.2

Text organisation
1. (a) use of words such as 'process,
        customer needs'
    (b) 'matching resources'
2. (a) first sentence of paragraph 2
    (b) product–market strategy

3. (a) both appear in the initial
        paragraph
    (b) to 'set the scene'; they announce
        a new topic

Comprehension
4. so products can be changed to match
    changing customer needs

5.

Internal	External
resources { human, physical	market conditions market opportunities competition

6. strategy = long-term and where to go
    tactics = short-term and how to get to
    where you are going

7. (a) product range development
    (b) product development
    (c) market development

Text 2.3

Skim and scan
    (a) increasing
    (b) Marks & Spencer

Comprehension
1. saves time; offers known features
2. (a) F, paragraph 1
    (b) T, paragraph 2
    (c) T, Table 2.3.1
    (d) T, Table 2.3.1
    (e) F, paragraph 2

3.

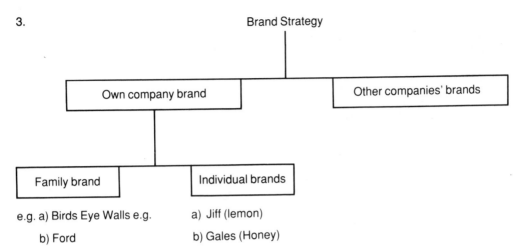

Brand Strategy

Own company brand

Other companies' brands

Family brand

Individual brands

e.g. a) Birds Eye Walls e.g.

b) Ford

a) Jiff (lemon)

b) Gales (Honey)

Vocabulary

4. (a) own label
   (b) corporate identity/corporate brand
   (c) product fields
   (d) sub-brand

5. (b) and (d)
6. itinerant = (b)
   anonymous = (d)
   compatible = (c)

7.

Verb	Noun	Adjective
represent	representation	X
associate	association	X
specify	specification	specifiable
rely	reliance reliability	reliable
identify	identification	identifiable
compare	comparison	comparable
dominate	domination	dominant

Viewpoint

8. = (b)
9. = (c)

Unit 3   Place

Text 3.1

Skim and scan

(a) 5
(b) The importance of place; The channel of distribution; Routes; Intermediaries; Why use intermediaries?

Comprehension

1. 'Place' is the means of getting the product to the right place at the right time.
2. (a) The importance of place, line 3, and the channel of distribution, lines 19–22
   (b) sales outlets for a travelling iron
   (c) loss of sales

3. (a) 2
   (b) trading route and physical route
   (c) trading route is to find buyers and the physical route is to move the product from producer to buyer.

4.

Advantages	Disadvantages
specialisation	loss of direct contact
economies of scale	loss of control
reduction in costs	

5.

CHEMICAL COMPANY   – – – = was using   SHOE COMPANY
                         ——— = is using now

Vocabulary

6. concentrate on   ignore
   lost   made
   convenient   inconvenient
7. outlets = definition 3
   handle = definition 3
8. quar = 4; quartet = a group of four; tele = across long distances; mis = wrong, false; miscalculation = mistakes, wrong thinking; inter = between; intermediaries = people who act between two other groups

Text 3.2

Pre-reading
A fad is something people are enthusiastic about briefly and then become bored with.
'Green' means conscious of and concerned about the environment.
To call someone green means they are naïve and have little experience.

Skim and scan
(a) company selling green and organic products
(b) Procter and Gamble — washing up liquids (Fairy Liquid) and washing powders (Ariel); Lever Brothers — washing powder (Persil)
(c) the time was right; consumer interest in green products
(d) growing — Dunn and Jones think it will quadruple

Comprehension
1. 'right product at the right time'; selling to supermarket buyers
2. no, they are the distributors
3. (a) he'd been a buyer for large supermarket stores
   (b) because he understood how buyers react and work
4. that interest in green goods is just a fad
5. there is product innovation and countries like Germany are influencing others regarding recycling, etc.; the '90s are supposed to be the caring, sharing decade
6. it is environmentally friendly
7. The distribution process is all about getting the right goods to the right place at the right time. An example of a success story in a very competitive area is that of the Ecover brands. They succeeded in breaking into the supermarket markets despite the strong position of brands such as Fairy Liquid, Ariel/Persil. This was partly a result of the time being right but also because of Jones' knowledge of the business and what supermarket buyers want, which is a winner. Ascot did not need to use any advertising to promote their products. It seems that the Green market is going to grow in the next few years.
8. the multiples = large chain stores
   this business = supermarket buying
   this = consumer interest in green goods
   this market = organic goods

Vocabulary
9. paragraph 2: tale = story; developed = emerged; many = a host of
   paragraph 3: seizing = grabbing
   paragraph 4: established = set up; previously = formerly
   paragraph 5: vital = crucial; using = recourse to
10. to hit the big time = be successful
    small beer = unimportant
    to be at loggerheads = in strong disagreement
    a passing fancy = short-term attraction
    to catapult = launch very rapidly

Text 3.3

Comprehension
1. it contains everything needed for consumption in the one packet
2. (a) spoon, napkin, the container for the milk, the wrapping round the sugar (and the box itself)
   (b) throw them away
3. convenience food
4. market segmentation, variety of products; the promotion of health and nutritional aspects

Vocabulary

6. (a) the box/pack(et)
    (b) to show surprise
    (c) to look at it carefully
    (d) the ground the players use, e.g. football pitch, hockey pitch, cricket pitch; area of activity

Text comparison

	Text 3.1	Text 3.2	Text 3.3
Source	textbook	magazine	magazine
Features	'our previous' section headings definitions figures rhetorical questions	short paragraphs quotes non-neutral vocabulary, e.g. 'dreaded supermarkets' idiomatic language, e.g. 'raise no eyebrows'	

Unit 4 Promotion

Text 4.1

Skim and scan

(a) 4
(b) advertising, personal selling, sales promotion, public relations
(c) you pay for advertising but not for the news items of public relations

Advertising

1. (a) paragraphs 1 and 2
    (b) several, including: unique qualities, positive
2. (a) final, paragraph 3
    (b) shortcomings, impersonal, cannot be as persuasive, very costly
3.

Positive features	Negative features
suggests standardisation and legitimacy repetition comparison expressive colourful mass appeal	impersonal less persuasive one-way only can be ignored expensive

4.

Column A	Column B	Column C
because of	due to	reason
yet	nevertheless	contrast
because	since	reason
also	moreover	addition
although	in spite of the fact that	contrast
in addition	additionally	addition

5. (a) = (iv)
    (b) long-term and short-term effects of advertising

6.

Adjective	Verb	Noun
general	generalise	generalisation
X	promote	promotion
standard	standardise	standardisation
legitimate	legitimise	legitimisation
popular	popularise	popularisation
persuasive	persuade	persuasion

Personal selling

7.

Positive features	Negative features
personal	time-consuming
interactive	expensive
cannot be ignored	less flexible

8. (a) paragraph 1
    (b) paragraph 1 ends with 'finally';
         new para: 'come at a cost'
9. (a) industrial goods (Figure 4.1)
    (b) because of a longer-term
         involvement than with consumer
         goods

10.

especially	particularly line 2
in comparison to	as compared with line 3
thus	so line 5
so as to	in order to line 9
even when	even if line 10

Sales promotion

11. (a) yes
     (b) yes
     (c) 'However'

12. (a) vouchers, competitions, money-off,
          extra quantity
     (b) free gifts, special offers, etc.

Public relations

13. (a) easily believed, reaches different
          people, does not seem like
          selling, dramatizes

     (b) not about PR itself; only that it is
          underused

Summarising

14. advertising; (a) to attract as many people as possible; (b) consumer goods
     personal selling: (a) establish personal contact; (b) large, expensive items
     sales promotion: (a) encourage quick response; (b) introducing a new product
     public relations: (a) reach different people; (b) new product

Text 4.2

Skim and scan

    (a) Fresh tea means the tea-leaves have been sealed within one day of picking; freshly brewed means water has just been poured on the tea-leaves.

    (b) Premier is the company; Typhoo is the product

    (c) Earl Grey is a special tea

Comprehension

1. (a) fresh tea
     (b) it is sealed from air within 24 hours
     (c) niche, i.e. specialist

2.

Promotional tool	Paragraph number	How it is being used
Advertising	5–7	to emphasise that this is a new concept
Personal Selling	3	create a new concept and image
Sales Promotion	5	samples to households
Public Relations	whole passage	to inform

3. (a) T, paragraph 1
     (b) F, paragraph 2: 'apart from water'
     (c) F, paragraph 5: £3m for marketing
     (d) T, paragraph 6
     (e) F, paragraph 9

Vocabulary

4. beverage = (c); tout = (d); genesis = (a)

5. extra price to be paid, i.e. 40 pence per 80 bags

Unit 5 Pricing

Text 5.1

Skim and scan

    (a) sulphuric acid
    (b) puts reliability of supply before price

Text organisation

1. paragraphs 1 and 2 making a claim
             3 justifying a claim
             4 giving an example
             5 stating a principle
             6 preparing for the next topic

Comprehension

2. (a) = (i)
     (b) 60% of DMUs would stay with the same supplier and not change even if 5–10% price cuts were offered.

3. (a) sulphuric acid
    (b) because sulphuric acid is
         corrosive and cannot be stored
         easily

4. (a) supply, quality and ease of
         ordering
5. (c)
6. (d), (b), (a), (c)

Vocabulary
7. (a) bulk = bought and sold in large
             quantities
    (b) commodity = product

8.

Verb	Adjective	Noun
supply	X	{ supplier supplies
sensitise	sensitive	sensation
continue	continual	continuation
prohibit	prohibitive	prohibition
corrode	corrosive	corrosion
produce	X	production

10. slit someone's throat
    bleed to death

Text 5.2

Skim and scan'
    (a) 4
    (b) F.W. Woolworth, Tiffany and Co., John Wanamaker, J.L. Hudson

Comprehension
1. = (b)
2. because large stores had too many
    employees to supervise bargaining
3. price provides revenue or income; the
    others are all costs
4. price
5. to make the most of changes in the
    market
6. Nowadays price is just one of the
    factors which influence a would-be
    buyer. While it will always be a
    consideration, quality, service,
    reliability, etc. may be equally or even
    more important considerations. Most
    goods are sold at a fixed price,
    although, particularly with large or
    repeat orders, some bargaining may
    be feasible. When bargaining a seller
    expects to lower the asking price and
    the buyer expects to raise the original
    offer.
    　　Pricing differs from the other 3 Ps
    because it results in revenue while the
    others all lead to costs. To price well
    you must continually review your
    price, you must relate it to your
    market strategy and be prepared to
    charge different prices in different
    market segments. In deciding on a
    price a company should not look only
    at cost.

Vocabulary
7. buyers/sellers, line 2; ancient/modern, line 5; small-scale/large-scale, line 6;
    employers/employees, line 9; revenue/costs, line 17; extrinsic/intrinsic, line 20;
    fixed/varied, line 21.
8. = (b)

Text 5.3

Skim and scan
  (a) vodka
  (b) 4
  (c) Heublien, 3 — Smirnoff, Relska, Popov; competitor, 1 — Wolfschmidt

Text organisation
1. Problem–Solution
2. See Part A in chart below.

Comprehension
3. (a) F, paragraph 1: claimed is not the same as stating/saying
   (b) T, paragraph 1: it could hold Smirnoff's price
   (c) T, paragraph 3: pretty much the same
   (d) F, paragraph 1: attacked is used metaphorically not literally

4.

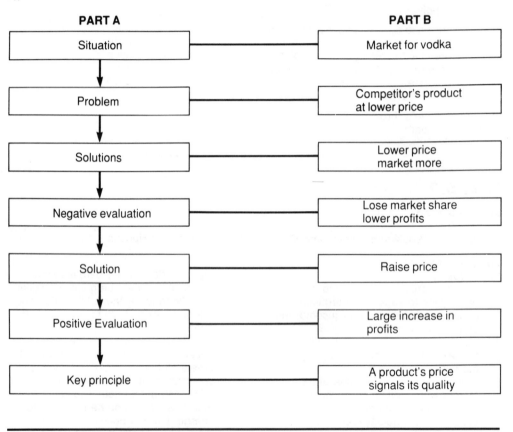

PART A	PART B
Situation	Market for vodka
Problem	Competitor's product at lower price
Solutions	Lower price market more
Negative evaluation	Lose market share lower profits
Solution	Raise price
Positive Evaluation	Large increase in profits
Key principle	A product's price signals its quality

Unit 6 Marketing services

Text 6.1

Pre-reading
goods = hamburgers, sportswear,
penicillin; services = hospitals, fast-food outlets, sportsclubs

Skim and scan
(a) 4
(b) intangibility, inseparability, perishability, heterogeneity

Comprehension
1. (a) can be physically possessed
   (b) cannot be physically possessed

2. (a) have the same aims
   (b) goods and services

3.

	Marketing problem	Service characteristic
(a)	quality control	heterogeneity
(b)	cannot be stored	perishability
(c)	simultaneous consumption and production	inseparability
(d)	quality control	heterogeneity

4.

Goods aspect	Services aspect
the car	the warranty
the food	the waitress's attention
the book	the cashier's behaviour
the pills	the doctor's time
spare parts	the quality and time taken

5. Traditional bakery: you are served personally so there may be conversation, advice and you may be able to place orders.

   Supermarket: you can take your own time, it can be quicker, pre-packaged product, limited choice.

Vocabulary
6. warranty = (d); nevertheless = (b); due to = (a); patents = (c); inventoried = (a).

7.

	Adverb	Adjective
(a)	simultaneously	simultaneous
(b)	concurrently	concurrent

Text 6.2

Pre-reading
art = painting, drawing, sculpture; the arts = drama, painting, poetry, music, dance, etc.

paintings—gallery, art museum; music—concert hall; drama—theatre

Skim and scan
(a) Victoria and Albert Museum
(b) advertising, public relations (this article), sales promotion (exhibitions, mailings, roadshow and club)

Comprehension
1. (a) F, paragraph 4: attempt to
   (b) T, paragraph 7
   (c) F, paragraph 9: talks about, wishes
   (d) T, paragraph 11, paragraph 5 + date of publication
2. (a) a controversial series of advertisements advertising the support service, the café, rather than the main service, the art objects
   (b) some reacted positively: paragraph 5, much loved; paragraph 7, attracted some. others reacted negatively: paragraph 5, loathed; paragraph 7, alienated

3.

Promotion technique	Target market
sales promotion: club	young working people
sales promotion: mailings	Asian community
sales promotion: roadshow	people in Leicester

4. museums and galleries

Viewpoint
5. (a) approve
   (b) paragraph 3, 'courageous'; paragraph 10; 'should congratulate itself'

Vocabulary
6. milestone = (a); fusty = (c); dumplings = (c)
7. place where tickets are sold
8. refreshes is used with reference to food and drink; i.e. this is a reference to the 'Ace caff' campaign increasing visitors to the V & A

Text 6.3

Skim and scan
(a) yes, as there is no exchange of goods; it deals with attitudes
(b) to create a celebrity — someone well-known
(c) widely-used

Text organisation

1. (i) definition; (ii) general examples; (iii) specific example; (iv) purpose; (v) specific characteristic; (vi) specific characteristic; (vii) process

Comprehension

2.

(a) Groups	(b) Aims
e.g. sports personalities, professionals, Drs, etc. charities	promote career increase income become well-known improve business increase contributions

3. (a) theming — focus on key benefits only
   (b) planning — especially timing
   (c) regionalisation — adapting speeches to suit particular groups
4. through careful planning of content plus timing of messages
5. (a and b) standard, Ronald Reagan = D; overnight, Lindbergh, Armstrong = B; comeback, Tina Turner, George Burns = F; meteor, William Perry = C
6. (a) Ronald Reagan
   (b) someone you know of well but your friends do not
   (c) Reagan

Vocabulary

7. get support; promote their careers; build reputations; sell policies; identify key issues;

8. = (d)
9. (a) peaks — declines; gains — loses; obscurity — fame
   (b) declines; achieved

Unit 7 International marketing

Text 7.1

Skim and scan

(a) to enter an unreceptive country
(b) Pepsi-Cola
(c) 6

Comprehension

1. (a) an Indian business group
   (b) domestic soft drinks companies and anti-multinational legislators
   (c) the government
   (d) getting into the Indian marketplace

2. (a) 5 — agriculture, rural economic development, food-processing, packaging, water-treatment
   (b) also, further

3. product, price, place, promotion, politics, public opinion

4.

	Company	Product	Special strategies
(1)	Pepsi	Pepsi-Cola	1. help with exports 2. help local economic development 3. provide technology
(2)	Olivetti	(office equipment)	1. builds houses 2. supports local arts and charities 3. trains local managers
(3)	IBM	(computers)	1. helps with nutrition programmes 2. gives agricultural advice
(4)	Polaroid	(cameras)	1. art restoration

Vocabulary

5. (a) very big; a million
   (b) (i) marketing on a large scale; (ii) device for making voices/sounds louder; (iii) believing you are very powerful

6. (a) gain the cooperation of
       offset the outlay
       seek approval for
       make an offer
       win the support of
       build good relations
   (b) gain and win
   (c) to seek = look for — you may be successful or unsuccessful; to win = you are successful
   (d) lose co-operation/support
       refuse an offer
       destroy good relations

Text 7.2

Skim and scan
(a) in America
(b) selection, entry, building and protection of market share
(c) Coca Cola; Schick; Polaroid; McDonald's

Comprehension
1. (a) skilful uses of marketing
   (b) management practices, help from the government, help from trading companies and banks, low wages, dumping (i.e. selling at less than cost price)
   (c) some, others, still others

2. (a) 5
   (b) adding new product lines, pricing more aggressively, streamlining production, buying/using non-American components, forming partnerships with foreign companies

3. computers, cameras
4. **Selecting markets:**
    industries requiring (skilled) personnel versus raw materials;
    common product design features;
    weak market leaders

    Entering markets:

Action	Purpose
1. evaluation	look for unfilled market niches
2. establish good distribution	provide quick service
3. advertising	gain consumer attention

    Main strategy = build market share versus make quick profits

    Building market share:
    develop new and better products;
    look for market segmentation and new countries;
    network markets and production

    Protecting market share:
    continuous product development and refining market segmentation

Vocabulary
5. developing good market share;
    dumping = selling at low (less than cost) prices; without all the extras;
    spend large sums of money

6. line up distribution channels; to build profits; to realise profits; to streamline production

---

Text 7.3

Pre-reading
foresight = looking ahead;
hindsight = understanding events after they have happened
Heinzight = the ability of Heinz to use past knowledge to predict events related to the company

spill the beans = tell something that people have been trying to keep secret
1992 = year of single European market

Skim and scan
(a) Europe
(b) UK
(c) Head of European operations
(d) 40

Comprehension
1. (a) T, paragraph 1: 25 years of unbroken profit
    (b) F, paragraph 2: one-third of £430m = £143m
    (c) F, paragraph 3: market penetration is too low

    (d) T, paragraph 5: hardly been unique
    (e) F, paragraph 6: over half = 20+

2.   (a) product range
     (b) company structure
     (c) decentralisation has been increased by some and decreased by others

     (d) there is now less difference between centralised and non-centralised, i.e. there is more of a middle structure with elements of both

Text organisation
3.   (a) particular (Heinz) to general (other companies)
     (b) good news (unbroken profit) to bad news (problem)
     (c) problem/need and then solution

Vocabulary
4.   (a) re = again; change
     (b) rethinking = think again and make a different decision
review = examine to see whether to make changes or not
restructure = to change the structure
redraw = to change

5.   4.2
6.   over-the-top = too enthusiastic, extravagant
too low for comfort = lower than it should be

Unit 8 Marketing and society

Text 8.1

Skim and scan
    (a) 3, including the one of societal marketing
    (b) only societal; the others share all the same concepts
    (c) 1984
    (d) in the 1950s

Comprehension
1.   it includes a concern for the overall welfare of society
2.   it does not take into consideration scarcity, (i.e. limitations in resources), the environment, population growth and economic factors such as inflation

Vocabulary
3.   rapid = with great speed;
explosive = with great speed and suddenly

Texts 8.2 and 8.3

Skim and scan

	Company	Good(s) produced	Material(s) used in manufacture
Text 8.2	BMW	vehicles/cars	precious metals, oil, rubber, plastics, steel, glass, leather, wood, fluids, acid, electronic parts
Text 8.3	AEG	electrical goods washing machines	steel, plastics, metals

Text 8.2

Comprehension
1. (a) F, paragraph 3
   (b) T, paragraphs 4 and 6
   (c) F, paragraph 8
   (d) F, paragraph 11
   (e) T, paragraph 12
   (f) T, paragraph 14
   (g) T, paragraph 15
2. (to learn) the most efficient dismantling techniques (and then to learn) how to design cars for total recycling
3. selecting recyclable materials, using non-toxic materials, identification scheme for plastics

Text 8.3

Comprehension
1.

	Group	Change needed
(a)	AEG employees	increased environmental awareness
(b)	suppliers	learn recycling qualities of materials
(c)	consumers	accept products which are recyclable

2. (a) downcycling = producing a low(er) grade material
   (b) finite market for low grade plastic/garden plant pots
3. (a) no
   (b) too serious an issue
4. (a) fifty; less; 1970
   (b) smaller; refrigerators; not; freezers
   (c) Japan; Europe

Vocabulary

5. scrap value
   life span
   waste disposal
   environmental awareness
   phosphate free
   reusable components

Combined questions

1. Text 8.2: paragraph 1
   Text 8.3: paragraph 3
2. energy efficiency
3. paragraph 2
4. in the diagrams
5. (a) T, paragraph 10 and paragraph
       19 (text 8.3)
   (b) F, paragraph 10 and paragraph
       14 (text 8.3)
   (c) T, paragraph 8 and paragraphs
       10, 19, 20 (text 8.3)
6. Recycling is being addressed seriously in Germany because of social and economic pressure but also because of new legislation that has been and is likely to be introduced. For example, it is probable that, by 1993, car manufacturers will have to recycle all the scrapped vehicles that originated on their production lines.

   BMW has built a pilot recycling plant in which scrapped cars are dismantled. Currently this takes about four or five hours but the aim is to design new cars so that the dismantling can be achieved in about one hour. A number of parts have been recycled for many years, particularly metal based ones and recently gasification has been introduced for oil, rubber, etc.

   A major problem remains with plastics where recycling is less well developed. As well as devising new processes so that highgrade plastics can be recycled without downgrading, companies, such as BMW and AEG, are looking at new design features. Goods will need to be designed so that they contain just one or a very limited number of different plastics and in such a way that the parts can be extracted without damage. While data is expected from the car recycling plant in just two years it will take at least ten for washing machine manufacturers to achieve results.

   conserving limited resources, i.e. scarcity, and environmental destruction

Text 8.4

Pre-reading
'No smoke without fire' is a saying which suggests that there is always an element of truth behind rumours.

Skim and scan
(a) that marketing is not the same as advertising; it is a much wider concept
(b) the power of branding and the need to combat not just promotion but the other Ps as well

Comprehension
1.

	For tobacco advertising	Against tobacco advertising
Reason/ belief	freedom of speech	wish to stop sales / harmful product
Weakness	not whether or not to advertise but what restrictions there should be	brands are too powerful; advertising alone does not sell goods

2.

	Price	Product	Place	Promotion
Action	increase	decrease size	ban public smoking limit sales outlets	restrict legislate re-packaging
Result of action	use extra funds for anti-smoking campaign	less appealing less tobacco	—	reduce sponsorship

Word partnerships

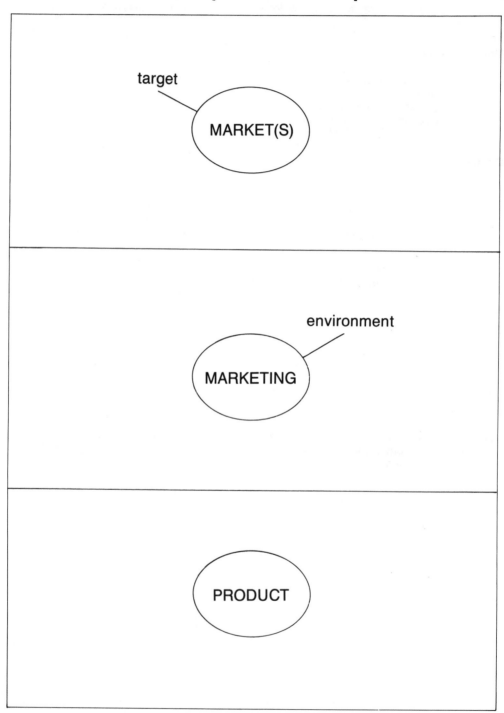

target

MARKET(S)

environment

MARKETING

PRODUCT

Word partnerships

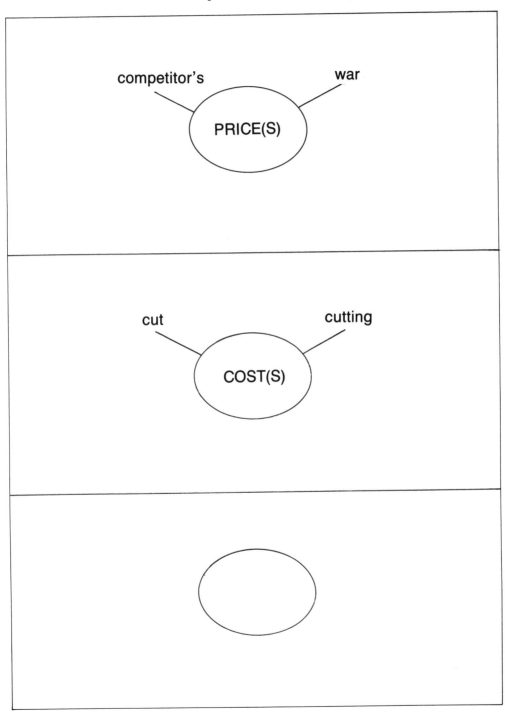

Word partnerships

Word partnerships

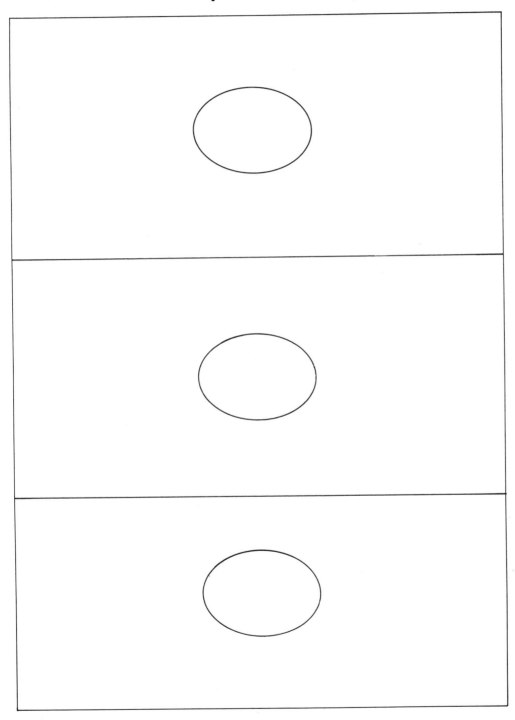

Word partnerships

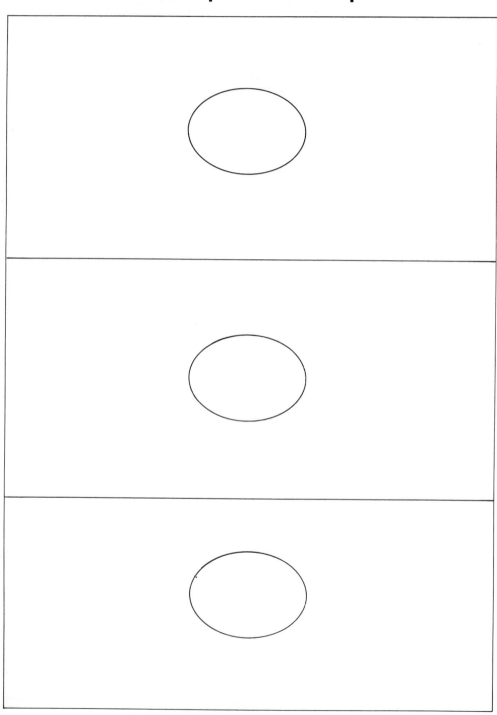

Word partnerships

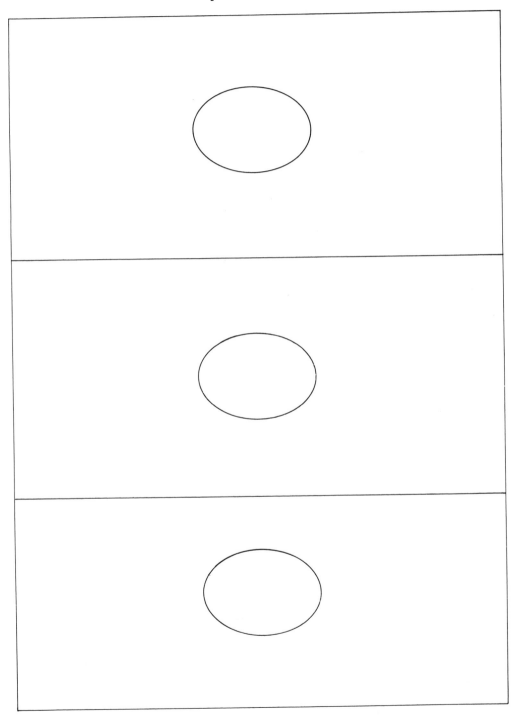